PUB WALKS
IN
Essex

PUB WALKS
IN
Essex

THIRTY CIRCULAR WALKS
AROUND ESSEX INNS

Norman Skinner

COUNTRYSIDE BOOKS
NEWBURY, BERKSHIRE

First Published 1993
Revised and updated 1995, 1998
© Norman Skinner 1993

COUNTRYSIDE BOOKS
3 Catherine Road
Newbury, Berkshire

ISBN 1 85306 235 9

Photographs and map designs by Ann Skinner
Cover illustration by Colin Doggett

Produced through MRM Associates Ltd., Reading
Typeset by Paragon Typesetters, Queensferry, Clwyd
Printed in England

Contents

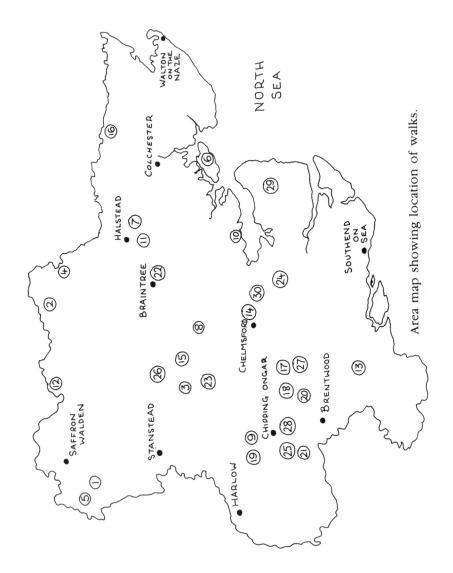

Area map showing location of walks.

Publisher's Note

We hope that you obtain considerable enjoyment from this book; great care has been taken in its preparation. However, changes of landlord and actual closures are sadly not uncommon. Likewise, although at the time of publication all routes followed public rights of way or well-established permitted paths, diversion orders can be made and permissions withdrawn.

We cannot accept responsibility for any inaccuracies, but we are anxious that all details covering both pubs and walks are kept up to date, and would therefore welcome information from readers which would be relevant to future editions.

Introduction

Essex is a surprisingly good county for walking. Yes, the landscape is not mountainous but, contrary to popular opinion, there is great variety of terrain, rolling hills, river meadows, and woodlands. In addition it has the longest coastline of any English county. Though stretching from the coast to the capital, Essex has an abundance of tiny villages, largely unspoilt by modern development. At the heart of many of these villages is the village pub, an institution in which for centuries the high and the lowly have swopped words over a pint of beer, and in so doing have helped to cement the parish structure. A more recent development has been the widespread provision of food in these establishments – some would say the English version of eating out which prevails in our EEC neighbour France. This book contains a selection of these pubs, and in each case a suggested short walk with which a visit to the hostelry could be combined.

Writing a book about walks from pubs seems a dream to someone like me who has spent a fair chunk of his spare time in pubs when indoors, and rambling when outdoors. It has been helpful that over the last 20 years I have spent most Sundays visiting pubs all over Essex in the course of days out walking. I must however clarify that the pubs in this book are not necessarily to be regarded as my choice of the best 30, though in fact I think many of them do fall into that category. Sometimes the selection was dictated by the location of an outstanding walk, sometimes a certain geographical spread was required which excluded otherwise well qualified candidates, and there were many excellent pubs which, while great as a lunch stop in the course of an all day ramble, were unsuitable bases for a short circular morning or afternoon stroll. Having said all that, most of these pubs are, in fact, my favourites and I am certain that all are well worth visiting.

The walks range in distance from 2½ miles to 6 miles with the majority being 3 to 4 miles, thus rendering them well within the compass of old and young alike. I have tried as hard as I can to make all the directions clear, on occasion selecting the more easily followed route. Experience tells me that for some there will be problems which I have not foreseen. I can only offer my apologies for this and trust, if you do go off course, that successfully regaining your route will enhance your self esteem. If not, you can always blame me.

The easiest time to walk in Essex is in the late summer and early autumn. Then the crops have all been cleared, the ground surface is usually firm, and the temperature is kind. Walking is, however, an all the year round pursuit for many and indeed the dry months of January and February are very enjoyable. The ground is usually crisp and, wearing suitable clothing, the activity will keep you warm. The spring brings warmer days but it also brings the rain, so good waterproof gear must be carried. In most pubs, muddy boots or shoes are definitely not welcome, and their presence can only damage the good reputation that walkers generally have. The solution is to carry a spare pair of shoes – or leave the boots outside and enter in your socks.

Finally a paradox: June and July sound like idyllic times to take a walk and so they are, sometimes. But in some years the combination of hot and dry followed by hot and wet weather promotes the abundant growth of bushes and weeds at this time, and paths which had been quite passable two months previously become blocked with thorns and nettles! Fortunately the 1990 Rights of Way Act is providing some improvement in this direction but it may be as well to carry a stick in these months. Again I have tried to route most of the walks away from potential problems of that sort.

It is advisable to carry a map in addition to the sketch map in the book, and the appropriate OS Landranger sheet is indicated for each walk. All but six of the walks are contained on Maps 167 or 168. You may wish to borrow these and the others, when needed, from the public library. I find a compass very useful combined with a map. It is not essential to carry one but from time to time I have included in the text general directions, and confirming these with a compass can be helpful.

I wish to pay tribute to my wife, Ann, for her encouragement and understanding. She is also responsible for the maps and photographs which are included. I do hope that this book will provide the reader with hours of pleasure. If I have enabled just a few people to get hooked on walking in the countryside, I will feel that it has been well worthwhile.

Norman Skinner

Arkesden
The Axe and Compasses

Arkesden (Arcell's valley) is a very pretty streamside village. The stream is called Wicken Water and it flows into the river Cam at Newport. The much celebrated soldier John Cutts, known to his men as 'The Salamander', described by Macauley as the bravest of the brave and who shone on the battlefields of the Duke of Marlborough, was born here in 1661.

The Axe and Compasses is a deservedly popular thatched village local. Opening hours are 11 am – 2.30 pm and 6 pm – 11 pm on Mondays to Saturdays. On Sundays it is open from 12 noon – 3 pm and 7 pm – 10.30 pm. A good choice of traditional pub food is available during these hours and there are some mouthwatering specialities – try their breast of duck in an oriental spicy sauce or supreme of chicken cooked in port and stilton. Sorry – food is available on Sunday evenings in the summer only.

Real ales on handpump are Greene King IPA and Greene King Abbott Ale. Taunton Blackthorn is on tap for draught cider lovers. Children are made welcome in the restaurant.

Telephone: 01799 550272.

How to get there: Coming from the south on the M11, leave at junction 8 to continue north on the B1383. Turn left in Newport on the B1038, signposted to Clavering. Just through Wicken Bonhunt turn right on a lane signposted to Arkesden, which is 1 ¼ miles further on.

Parking: Park at pub car park. You may leave your car while you walk but do ask the landlord first.

Length of the walk: 4½ miles. OS Map Landranger series 154 Cambridge and Newmarket (GR 483344).

Oh what a lovely walk! Clavering is well known for its many attractions. In juxtaposition Arkesden sheltering in the winding valley is possibly the prettiest village in the vicinity. Our walk explores the countryside connecting these two.

The Walk

At the pub door turn left along the main street for 130 yards. Now turn left at a concrete footpath sign to climb out of Arkesden. Look back for a good view of the church, another of those which appear to be too big for their villages. With Norman foundations and a 15th century tower the building is mainly 700 years old. You reach the woods at the top of the hill and, appropriately enough, Wood Hall is on your left. Scholars, however, say it is derived from Wode Hall and quite old – 17th century. Cross a well-defined path and keep going south. Fork right for a few yards then continue with a hedge on your left. At the corner of the field go into a dark hole in the hedge with a deep ditch on your left and in a few yards turn right to emerge by a concrete footpath post onto the village green at Stickling Green.

Turn left along the road for 250 yards. Here at a concrete bridleway sign turn right along Colehill Lane. In ½ mile you reach Clavering ('the place where clover grows'). On your left is the Fox and Hounds pub. Cross a little wooden bridge to turn right up the road. In a few yards you turn right again into a very pretty part of the village. This leads to the church with the remains of Clavering Castle behind. The church is 14th century, an age of confidence and prosperity. Placed among the first four churches of north west Essex, it has one of the best of Essex roofs and a screen outstanding for its light and grace. Look out for the Jacobean oak pulpit, carved on each of its seven panels, with delicate inlay work of other woods. In the churchyard you may see an ash and a maple growing out of a massive tomb, which commemorates two persons by the name of Hewitt. The female Hewitt said when living 'If there is a heaven and a hell an ash and a maple will grow above my grave'. According to which grew out of the tomb so would she be in heaven or hell. The ash has strangely split her tomb, so we assume she is in paradise.

The castle was that rarity, a pre-Conquest castle established by Norman immigrants under Edward the Confessor and it made Clavering a place of importance in the Middle Ages. The walls which topped the earthworks have now quite gone but from the back lane you can cross a stream and walk among the low embankments.

When your sightseeing is complete retrace your steps from the church into Middle Street to cross the bridge at the ford. Just over the road take the path by the footpath sign and walk along a waymarked

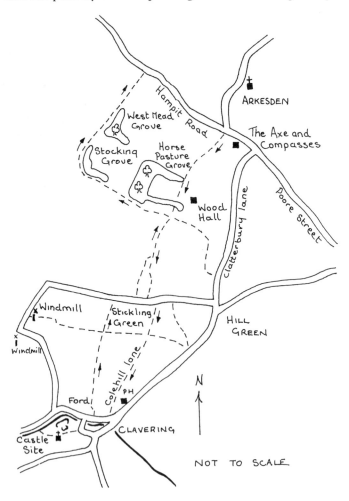

path over a stile to a field. The path is usually defined between the crops and you walk northwards till you reach the back gardens of Stickling Green. Over to your left are two attractive windmills, though the sails have gone. Almost opposite the end of the path is a way between two hedges which leads you out to the village green. Cross the road and bear right to the footpath sign you came to on your outward journey. From here retrace your steps for ½ mile till you reach the crossing track at the woods. Turn left along this track by Horsepasture Grove and Stocking Grove.

At the corner cross a double plank bridge and turn right, with woods and hedge on your right. This grove is called Knock'emdown! Past Westmead Grove the route is all downhill to the road. Here is a redundant Methodist church accompanied by several cottages with strong names – Shepherds, Mynchins, Heddas, Finns, and Ancient Shepherd. Turn right and walk for about 700 yards back to the Axe and Compasses in Arkesden.

Belchamp St. Paul
The Half Moon Inn

Belchamp St. Paul is the largest of the three Belchamps, but with all that having only a population of a few hundred. There is a wide attractive village green, and about a mile distant the church and Paul's Hall have kept themselves company for 500 years. One of the Golding family who inhabited the hall was Arthur Golding, who was born 30 years before Shakespeare but outlived him. He wrote translations of the classics, and these were of great value to Shakespeare who, it seems, used other people's stories instead of inventing his own.

The Half Moon Inn is a beautiful thatched 16th century building. Opening hours are 11.30 am-2.30 pm and 7 pm-11 pm, Mondays to Saturdays, 12 noon-3 pm and 7 pm-10.30 pm on Sundays. Food is served 12 noon-2 pm and 8 pm-10 pm but not on Sunday evenings or Monday evenings. The food is all home-made and specialities include pork fillet with cream sauce and roast rack of lamb. The more adventurous may like to try the habachi grill – a sort of table top barbecue for meats and sweets. A freehouse, the real ales on tap are Greene King IPA and Nethergate Bitter and IPA. Draught Strongbow cider is also available. Children are welcome and there is a children's menu. As if this were not enough the Half Moon is haunted but not during opening hours!

Telephone: 01787 277402.

How to get there: Travel on the A604 north though Sible Hedingham. Turn off right in the middle of Great Yeldham and follow the signs to Tilbury and Clare. At Tilbury Court go straight on, signposted to Belchamp St. Paul. The Half Moon is in the centre of the village opposite the green.

Parking: At the pub. There should be no problem about leaving your car while you walk but please ask first.

Length of the walk: 3½ miles. OS Map Landranger series 155 Bury St. Edmunds and Sudbury Area (GR 792423).

The experts tell me that this is one of the best little walks in the book. There is some up and down, lots of tranquillity, views and the choice (if you want) of no less than two additional pubs!

The Walk

Leaving the pub turn left and walk up the long green, stopping to work out how the water pump worked. You pass some interesting houses on your right including St. Paul's Place. Next door is an old garage and just past this on your right the entrance to bridleway 27. Walk down a long green lane some 15 feet wide with a ditch on either side. Glimpse a distant farm at the far edge of the field on your right. The quiet is disturbed only by birdsong. At the end of the green lane the bridleway turns right. You turn a little to the left passing a red 'no horses' sign with the hedge on your left. At the hedge corner take a line across the field to the next corner. Then follow a second diagonal line across the second field. This path is well walked by local doggy walkers and is easy to follow as it passes under the power lines. The views here are onward to Ovington and Ovington Hall, and to the right, Butlers Farm.

Join the hedge path beside the ditch on your left and walk south along this well-trodden headland. Go through the hedge line when you reach it and head half right downhill across the field to the trees. At the edge of this field make your way carefully ahead over some tree roots on the visible route through trees to an unusual bridge. This is made from old telegraph poles with eight stepping treads, a very firm and secure crossing into a long, narrow field. Continue ahead to the

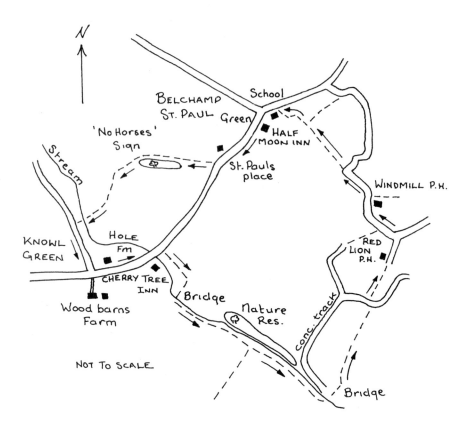

road and footpath sign 28. Turn left along the narrow country lane ignoring the concrete track on your right to go uphill. You pass the Knowl Green village sign. At the T junction turn left and pass the post box opposite Hole Farm.

Go downhill past the Cherry Tree Inn. Cross over a stream and come to a footpath sign on the right. Turn along this path with the stream across a field. At the end of the first field turn right following waymarks to the corner. Turn left to a bridge and cross this, turning left with the stream on your left alongside. At the end of this field cross over a plank bridge and continue with the stream on your left. Enjoy the sounds of the wind rustling the leaves and the birds overhead in the peace of the countryside, unaltered here for so many years.

When you come to a nature reserve you will want to identify the six or more species of trees. Ignore the concrete track to the left and continue under the oak tree till you come to a metal bridge. Go over this bridge. The path crosses a concrete track and runs up the field (north east) to a farm road corner. The farmer marks the line of this path but, when necessary, local walkers, after crossing the bridge turn left along the concrete track and follow this track to reach the same point. Just to the west of the farm road corner and to the west of the hedge, there is an earth bridge into a wide grassy area, leading to a red tiled old stable building and passing a pond on your right. Note the waymark at the end of the garden ahead and go to the right of the house to join a made up road and pass the Red Lion, our third pub on the walk! If all three are visited the walk may take some time to complete. At the end of Fowes Lane turn left along the road passing another pond on your left and Windmill House on your right.

Continue down the road passing the Belchamp Otten sign, ignoring the footpath sign on the right. At a bend in the road leave the road, walking on well-cut grass with a garage on your left and a house on your right. Follow the headland path under the power lines. Now head for the timber farm buildings. Go through the gap in the hedge ahead. Keep the hedge on your left and reach the road beside the farm buildings. Walk along this road for a few yards till the road bends to the right. At this point turn left on a well-mown track. Cross the hedge line and turn right, keeping a wood on your right. At the end of this field turn left and then right to follow a path to the right of a school fence. As you spot the wooden duck sign for the Belchamp St. Paul school nature reserve, turn right to cross the concrete bridge and walk out to the road at footpath 10, turn left and soon you reach the Half Moon.

Bishop's Green
The Spotted Dog

The Spotted Dog has for many years been popular with ramblers, for the friendly welcome it has given, its geographical location at the centre of a varied footpath network, and the very tranquillity of its garden. Opening hours are from 11 am-3 pm and 6 pm-11 pm on Mondays to Saturdays, 12 noon-3 pm and 7 pm-10.30 pm on Sundays. A changing variety of meals are on offer daily, as well as a children's menu. Always available is a modestly priced roast dinner.

Three real ales are on tap: Bass, Greene King IPA and a guest beer. There is also sweet or dry draught Bulmers cider. The restaurant area is open to children with adults, as is the garden into which dogs on leads can also go. The landlord is even willing for walkers to eat their own food in the garden providing a drink or a coffee is purchased at the bar.

Telephone: 01245 231598.

How to get there: Bishop's Green is about 2 miles from Barnston along the High Easter Road, and Barnston is about 2 miles south east of Great Dunmow on the A130.

Parking: You may leave your car in the pub car park, but please ask first.

Length of the walk: 2½ miles. OS Map Landranger series 167 Chelmsford and Harlow (GR 631179).

An attractive short walk but with pretty features. First the bridge which was won by the Ramblers in 1989 after years of begging. The track down to Roffeys is delightful. Do persevere with the crossfield paths to Mountain's Farm for the wide green track up towards Garnetts Wood is superb. Finally it is always a great joy to stroll through Garnetts. The whole walk will probably not take much more than an hour.

The Walk

Leave the pub and cross the road towards the black footpath sign on your left. Turn right along the field edge with the hedge on your right. Continue until you see the railings of the river bridge slightly to your left. Cross the bridge with care to avoid hitting your head on the tree that leans against the bridge as a result of the gales. The path now crosses a wide green lane and a second path joins from the right. Your route continues ahead past the edge of a wild area with a pond and onwards to the road. At the road turn right, noting the back of the farm buildings opposite the Spotted Dog and later Garnetts Wood in the distance. When you get to a black metal gate turn left on the gravel track beside a field. Keep the hedge on your left and the ditch on your right as you go gently downhill.

This is a good point to survey the route ahead. You can see directly in front of you the roofs of Roffey Farm. The land to the right dips down till it forms a channel for Martel's Brook that runs from the spring near Martel's Manor. Beyond the brook the land rises again and to the right of Roffey Wood you can see the distinctive buildings of Mountain's Farm. Further to the right the cluster of buildings in the distance is Barnston village.

Having now a good idea of the route to be followed, continue down the track until you reach Roffey Farm. Turn right behind the second barn with a hedge on your left. Leaving the buildings cross a field to the left edge of Roffey Wood. Pass with the wood on your right and cross a plank bridge over the ditch. Now cross the next field, to the lane left of a white house. Turn right and pass to the south of Mountain's Farm. A good track leads down to the tiny brook (wooden bridge) and uphill. At the first field the bridge is missing, but it's not too difficult to cross. At the third field bear right and follow the edge with a hedge on your right. The exit from this field involves negotiation of barbed wire – regretfully the necessary stile is not in

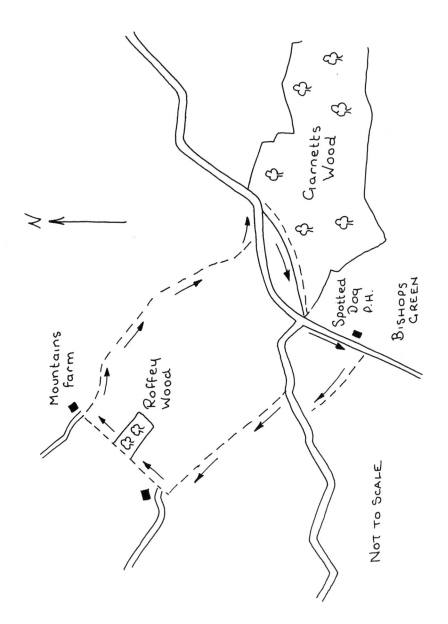

N

Garnetts
Wood

Spotted
Dog
P.H.

BISHOPS
GREEN

Mountains
farm

Roffey
Wood

NOT TO SCALE

20

place. The road area is full of interest. As you turn left note the arch made by the trees on the road. Continue down the road until you reach the car park at Garnetts Wood.

At the back of the car park you will see the gate with the intriguing notice carefully sculptured to form a novel Essex County Council sign. This also carries the warning 'No Horses'. Cross the stile just to the right of the gate and enter Garnetts Wood. The tracks immediately divide. Take the track to the right at the edge of the wood. Because of the recent forestry work undertaken in this area you will be able to enjoy a feast of nature. On recent visits I have seen a wide range of flowers, some butterflies, and listened to lots of different birds as they serenaded me on my way. This is quite my favourite part of the walk.

All too soon the path turns left and a gate and stile to the right lead out of the wood and back to the road. Turn left, noting the interesting extension to the white bungalow. Then you pass a small lake on your left and a farm pond on your right. You may find a range of fruit for sale in the farm. Anything to tempt a passing walker today? Just to your left you will find your waiting car.

Perhaps another day you will return to explore Garnetts Wood, parking at the ECC car park. If you do, take careful note of your directions as this small wood can bamboozle the unwary.

Lamarsh
The Red Lion

Lamarsh church is one of six in Essex with round towers, and only three of which were built in Norman times. The odd looking spire with its little dormer windows is modern, but one of the lancet windows is 12th century. Back along the road towards Sudbury is Daw's Hall surrounded by fine trees and a nature reserve has been established here. The Hall at Lamarsh is hidden from the road behind a farmyard, its striking timbered south front facing a pretty pond.

The Red Lion at Lamarsh is an attractive pub whose owners are justifiably proud of the food and drink which they serve. The beers are cosmopolitan in that Suffolk provides Porter's Suffolk Bitter and Adnam's Broadside, and Alsaçe, Kronenbourg 1664. Blackthorn cider comes from the can. We found the food excellent with the usual, good sandwiches, and for main course, chicken and ham pie, lasagne, or scampi and at any time the Big Breakfast. Part of the building dates back to 1305 and the bar is constructed of wooden screens from a church. The garden rises steeply from the road and at the top there is a magnificent view over the river Stour to Suffolk. The landlady welcomes dogs in the bar providing they behave and young children can come in to the restaurant to eat lunch. The hours are 11 am-3 pm and 6 pm-11 pm Monday to Saturday, 12 noon-3 pm and 7 pm-10.30 pm Sunday.

Telephone: 01787 227918.

How to get there: Take the B1508 Sudbury road from Bures and after a mile at the start of Lamarsh arrive at the Red Lion.

Parking: At the pub. Please ask permission to leave your car before setting out on your walk.

Length of the walk: 3 miles. OS Map Landranger series 155 Bury St. Edmunds and Sudbury area (GR 892355).

This is a pleasant walk to the attractive village of Alphamstone, giving good views over the Stour valley.

The Walk

Leave the Red Lion and turn left along the road. Pass some houses and turn right and left. At the corner of the Alphamstone Road take note of a lovely thatched house. Walk up this road after turning left. Here there is a mixture of fine, old houses, some thatched and more modern dwellings. After 250 yards, opposite a cottage known as the Long Thatch, turn left at a concrete footpath post and climb up the side of a large field, part of the 'set aside' land. The path climbs and bears to the right keeping to the side of a wood. When you reach a waymark arrow pointing left into the wood turn right and cross over the field to the edge of the wood opposite. Here take in the magnificent views over the Stour valley and beyond in Suffolk to the north east. Continue downhill by the edge of the wood.

At the bottom cross a stream in a thicket by walking on a pipe and then proceed steeply uphill to a field edge. The path goes straight on across a field but local walkers turn right on a good grassy path to go round the field edge to reach the point where you turn right out of the field by a good path to the church at Alphamstone. This is a very attractive village, one of several in this area between Bures and Sudbury. After passing the church, cross the road into a narrow lane and immediately turn left by a concrete footpath post. Bear left again to the drive leading to Dyne House. Just past the building turn left at a footpath mark and climb some steps. Turn right along a path between a fence and a row of trees. Through trees turn right along a field edge with a fence on your right. At a waymark arrow turn left across the field

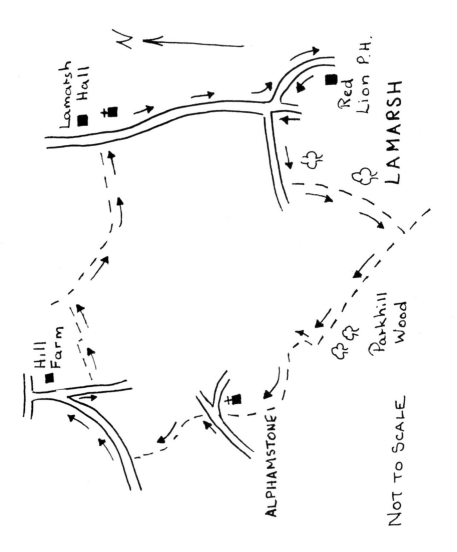

N

Lamarsh Hall

Red Lion P.H.

LAMARSH

Parkhill Wood

Hill Farm

ALPHAMSTONE

NOT TO SCALE

to a plank bridge over a steep ditch. Cross the bridge and continue straight on to the far corner. Go through a hedge gap and steeply uphill to the lane by a concrete footpath post. Turn right and walk down the lane through trees and uphill to a T junction. Turn right past Hill Farm House. At the concrete footpath sign turn left over a stile and walk across the field to a stile to the right of a metal gate. These fields are home to a herd of cattle and in the field to the right a large number of free range pigs roam. At the end of this field cross a stile and turn right along a ridge path with views over the parish of Lamarsh and the Stour Valley. Later a waymark points left downhill to Lamarsh Hall and the church. This is a fine, steep downhill path and you reach the Bures road by a concrete footpath post. It is worth a close look at the round tower of the church before walking along the side of the road back to Lamarsh village to a warm welcome at the Red Lion.

Duddenhoe End
The Woodman

Essex place names are nothing if not entertaining. The Duddenhoe in Duddenhoe End is probably a variation of the name of the person who farmed Duddenhoe Grange in the 12th century. The village is in the parish of Wenden Lofts. Wenden like nearby Wendens Ambo describes a winding valley. Lofts you may think of as Upper Wendens, but no – the experts say it comes from Robert Louhot who owned land there in 1236, and of course we have the church and Lofts Hall not much more than a mile from Duddenhoe End.

The Woodman was a beerhouse as long ago as the 16th century. Now a freehouse, it is surprisingly spacious with a long bar to serve the former public and saloon bar areas, and a games/children's room. The previous owner had an old parrot in a cage in the corner, and the tradition is being continued with a younger successor. Opening hours are 12 noon-3 pm, Monday to Saturday and 12 noon-3 pm on Sundays. Evening times are 6.30 pm-11 pm Monday to Friday, and 7 pm-10.30 pm on Sundays. Food is available throughout opening times and is traditional pub fare, mostly home-made. A speciality dish is Woodman chicken marinated in rosemary.

For the real ale lovers Cheltenham Flowers IPA and Adnams Extra are on offer plus a' guest beer which varies each month. No less than three draught ciders are served: Strongbow, Scrumpy Jack, and Red Rock. Families may 'wine and dine' in the children's room; but dogs may only 'dine' in the garden, which is now situated in front of the building (the old garden is the car park). The Woodman is a fine old building with an extension and is well worth a visit.

Telephone: 01763 838354.

How to get there: Coming from the south on the M11 leave at junction 8 to continue north on the B1383. After pasing through Newport, at the signs for Audley End station turn left on the B1039. After about 4 miles turn left again on a minor road to follow the signposts to Duddenhoe End. You will turn right off this road and drive through the village to find the Woodman.

Parking: Park in the pub car park but please ask the landlord before embarking on your walk.

Length of the walk: 4 miles. OS Map Landranger series 154 Cambridge and Newmarket (GR 460367).

It's not often that you can tell your friends that you have climbed to the roof of Essex. This walk will entitle you to do that but it will also introduce you to some beautiful countryside far from the madding crowds. With not a lot of effort you can spend a couple of hours making the acquaintance of the western borders of the county. The options are endless.

The Walk

Turn right after leaving through the pub garden. On reaching a T junction turn left and walk along the road signposted to Langley. You pass a sizeable pond on your left and reach Duddenhoe End Farm on the right. This house is impressive with substantial gardens to the south. Two hundred yards further on you come to the drive leading to White Friars Farm. Walk up this drive. Soon you will see a rather unusual white plastic sign indicating with a squiggly arrow that the path continues on the other side of the right hand hedge. Sure enough there is a gap in the hedge and you can pass through. Now turn left and follow for 250 yards the field edge with the hedge on your left. At the field corner two substantial plank bridges convey you over two ditches to the next field. You continue your previous direction aiming about 75 yards to the left of a small wood at the field boundary opposite. When you reach it look for a narrow gap and walk through into Lorking's Lane, an old unmade up road, now a grass track. These abound in this district, some are of Roman origin but all must go back hundreds of years. When you find this one turn right and make your way past the wood to a road. Turn left and follow the road round right and left hand bends for ½ mile to Langley Upper Green. You pass Duddenhoe Grange Farm on the right then soon after a football ground with fitted floodlighting. I can remember in the fifties when even some of the richest football clubs were not floodlit. Now Langley Upper Green is!

Finally you arrive at a house named 'Wickets' on the left. It has an interesting ceramic sign. Here turn right past the Community Centre and walk north west between the village green on the left and some large modern houses on the right. In amongst these is a very old farm house with most unusual chimneys. At this point you may wish to visit Langley Hall and church. If so turn left and walk over the delightful green to the road. Soon turn right off the road to follow a path to the church. The nave has kept its Norman doorway whilst the chancel is Tudor. The hall is from the time of Cromwell, but the ensemble with its elevated position stands proudly looking west to nearby Hertfordshire.

To continue the walk regain your position across the village green on the gravel path and walk north west towards a scrub area. At a tree stump the way continues with a just visible path leading over the scrub for 200 yards to a narrow gap in the hedge facing you. Go through this and turn right to follow the field edge, soon turning left. When you reach the end of the hedge at a wide gap turn right uphill to Oldfield Grove. Here you have reached 482 ft, and though this is not some towering mountain top it is nevertheless the highest point in Essex. Turn left and follow the field edge for 80 yards to enter and cross diagonally the narrow wood. Now walk north east with another strip of woodland on your left.

The way later becomes a wide grass track and you slowly descend for over ¾ mile to the fine farmhouse building of Chiswick Hall. The views are considerable on the way, especially those of Chrishall church. You pass on your right the vast High Wood. When you reach Chiswick Hall farm buildings, walk past a black corrugated building, turning slightly right for a few yards. Now turn right almost at right angles to walk south east downhill towards Mead Bushes Wood. Find and cross a metal railed bridge. Cross a farm track and turn uphill along the line of the wood. A deep ditch separates the field from the wood.

At the end of the wood turn half left and aim straight for the projecting corner of the wood ahead. At this corner walk east along the wide grass track, still with the wood on your left to the end of the

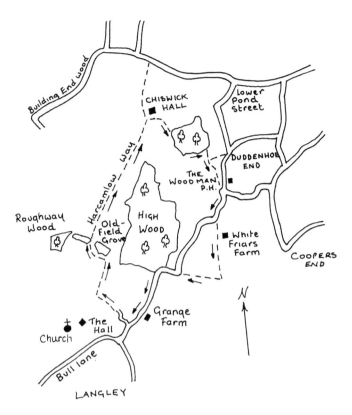

LANGLEY

NOT TO SCALE

field. Pause here – you are going to turn right down a wide grass track, but first walk into the next field for a great view to your left of Lofts Hall and church, and below them the tiny cluster of houses at Lower Pond Street. To the east is the extensive vista over this lovely part of Essex. It was once described as 'The East Anglian Heights'! Now come back to the previous field and walk south, soon to reach a substantial bridleway bridge by a spindly ash tree.

Walk over the bridge and turn half left to cross a narrow field (south east). Reach the field corner by a gnarled tree stump. Cross over the earth bridge. If the path has not been reinstated follow the field edge to your left towards a delightful thatched cottage and garden, then turning right to reach a gap in the hedge on your left by a footpath sign. Cross this and walk the few yards to the right, back to the Woodman and your car.

East Mersea
The Dog and Pheasant

Mersea is a genuine island although the causeway which connected it at low tide has been boosted to the point of nearly always being passable. The busier end is the west, but East Mersea, though more occupied in the summer than it was, still retains its rustic charm. Those who have lived here include the Romans, the Saxons, and the Danes. 'A patch of loveliness', said Arthur Mee.

The Dog and Pheasant is in a 20th century building, but the curious fact is that the previous building dating from 1750 stands behind and to the side of it. Owned previously by Truman, Hanbury and Buxton, the Dog and Pheasant is now a freehouse with a mixed clientele of locals and visitors to the island. As for all those Romans that were about, the inn contains no spirits other than liquid ones!

Opening hours are 12 noon-3 pm and 6 pm-11 pm, Mondays to Saturdays and 12 noon-3 pm and 7 pm-10.30 pm on Sundays. Food is available seven days a week but not after 2 pm or 9.30 pm. On

Sundays there is always a reasonably priced roast dinner, and the menu lists a good variety of traditional pub fare. A speciality is the availability of several varieties of sausages.

The landlord offers real ale and concentrates on quality. When I was there it was Greene King IPA. In addition a guest beer is usually on tap. Draught Stowford Press cider from Herefordshire is also available. Children (over 14) are welcome to eat in the bar, and there is a garden which will suit the younger set.

Telephone: 01206 383206.

How to get there: You must get on the B1025, via Peldon from the west and south, via Abberton from the north. Now follow the signs to Mersea crossing The Strood, a very ancient causeway, to reach the island. Keep left when the road forks and reach the Dog and Pheasant in 2½ miles.

Parking: At the pub. Please ask at the bar however so that the landlords know they haven't inherited a strange car!

Length of the walk: 4½ miles. OS Map Landranger series 168 Colchester and the Blackwater (GR 055146).

There's something about an island, even one as near the mainland as Mersea. This walk is mainly around the eastern end of the island – an idyllic spot. To marry this with the inland delights of the wildside walk to get there and the unique route past the church on the way back makes this walk one to do and then take your friends on.

The Walk

From the pub turn left and then left again into Shop Lane. Continue down the lane passing a chicken farm on your left between the bends, and interesting little cottages and bungalows as the road drops down the hill. Eventually you round a right hand bend and see a notice ahead. 'No Road. Access only.' Ignore this and turn left where you see the sign 'Dowsings' to pass a footpath sign rather hidden behind an ivy covered tree on your left. You walk on a gravel track with grass in the centre as you pass 'The Saltings' on your right. The scent from the pine wood on your left is most refreshing.

As the track swings right, you climb over a two step stile on your left. Note the well constructed dog access built into this stile. The path goes through a wooded section and you dip under an ivy covered bough and climb a slope over what appears to be an old shelter before dropping back to ground level on the other side. Take care on these slopes, in wet weather they can be slippery. The pine wood continues on your left as you cross a wooded area to leave by a plank bridge.

31

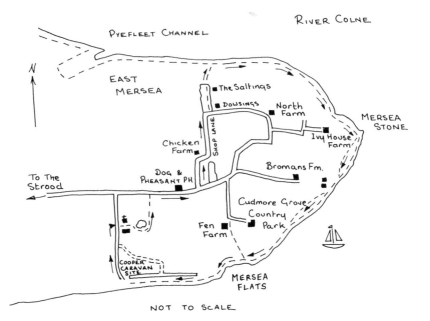

RIVER COLNE

PYEFLEET CHANNEL

N

EAST MERSEA

The Saltings

Dowsings

North Farm

MERSEA STONE

SHOP LANE

Chicken Farm

Ivy House Farm

Dog & Pheasant PH

Bromans Fm.

To The Strood

Cudmore Grove Country Park

Fen Farm

COOPER CARAVAN SITE

MERSEA FLATS

NOT TO SCALE

Look out for a 3 ft post with yellow arrows and the green countryside badge. The route now follows to the right of a ditch. This pleasant grass track leads to a second two step stile with another dog gate.

Climb up onto the sea wall ahead and then stop for a while to admire the view. In front of you is Pyefleet Channel, once famous for oysters, and to your left Peldon church rises from the distant hill in the west. Over to the east, Brightlingsea is a cluster of houses, and, between, the river Colne meets the sea in Brightlingsea Reach. Now follow the sea wall towards Brightlingsea. The sea wall walk from here to Cudmore Grove Country Park has a character all of its own. There is a great variety and of course you walk east, south, and west.

As you approach Mersea Stone you see the red roofs of Ivy House Farm on your right. The far river bank is highlighted by the brightly painted beach huts, the red marker buoy bounces brightly in midstream, the birds sweep overhead. The yellow sand on the beach shows up in the marsh, whilst the dyke on the right again marches in line with the sea wall. Here you may wish to tarry a while. Often in the past we have walked here and enjoyed a dip in the sea. You can continue the walk on the sea wall or later on follow the beach below.

When the two routes meet keep along the seashore. Soon your route may not be easy. Climb back up to the clifftop and walk along behind the trees for 300 yards then make your way back to the beach.

After ¾ mile you reach a site packed with holiday homes of various vintages, culminating in a large clubhouse. Just beyond this look for a footpath sign and turn right with it to follow a concrete track for 700 yards passing the Cooper caravan site to arrive at East Mersea church, standing splendidly on its low hill. Sabine Baring-Gould was rector here from 1871 to 1881 and he wrote 'Mehala', a stirring tale of the Essex salt marshes.

Turn right in front of the church and walk through a grassy area with the churchyard on your left and a long red brick barn on your right. On the right hand side of the cottage facing you there is an open building with a grey slate roof and at the back of this building is a pair of high wooden doors. Lo! and behold, they open by sliding aside the wooden fasteners. Was it the same carpenter who made the dog doors? At all events rejoice and pass through into the garden remembering to fasten the doors. Walk on to negotiate a two step stile. The path passes a large pond and onwards north to a bridge and stile in the hedge by the main road. Here turn right for 400 yards to reach the Dog and Pheasant.

Ford Street
The Shoulder of Mutton

Ford Street lies roughly midway between the villages of Fordham and Aldham. It is mainly south of the river Colne thus part of Aldham parish. However the Shoulder of Mutton and a few other dwellings flank the road north of the river and are in the Parish of Fordham. Formerly the road did not cross the river at this point so presumably there was a ford for horse drawn traffic. Hence Ford Street. Another suggestion is that Ford comes from Robert de la Forde who lived here in the 13th century. Perhaps both theories are correct? Or neither? Suffice to say that there must have been reasons why these fine houses grouped together at Ford Street, not to mention the three pubs, for there is no school and no church. If the patrons of the Shoulder of Mutton were often travellers waiting for the waters of the flooding river to ebb, they certainly picked a fine building to wait in. The present building goes back to the 15th century and there is evidence of an inn on the site 700 years ago.

The Shoulder of Mutton is a former Ind Coope house, now run by the Pubmaster company. Opening hours are 12 noon-2.30 pm and 6 pm-11 pm on Mondays to Saturdays, 12 noon-3 pm and 7 pm-10.30 pm on Sundays. Food is available every day during these hours, but cutting off at lunchtime at 2 pm. Various hot dishes are available from scampi to steaks. Ever popular are home-made soup and a ploughman's.

On the real ale front there is Ind Coope Bitter, Tetley Bitter, and a guest beer which is normally either Greene King IPA or Cheltenham Flowers. A very attractive garden extends between the pub and the river.

Telephone: 01206 240464.

How to get there: Leave the A12 at the A120 turn off and make for Marks Tey station, also signposted to Aldham. After 1½ miles pass Aldham church closely on your right. Soon you will reach a T junction. Turn left onto the A604. In a few yards cross the bridge over the river Colne and the Shoulder of Mutton is on your right.

Parking: Park at the pub but please ask the landlord before leaving your car to go on the walk.

Length of the walk: 3 ¾ miles. OS Map Landranger series 168 Colchester and the Blackwater (GR 920271).

This walk is on good wide paths and tracks throughout. This is partly because it is often on the route of the Essex Way, and partly because the farmer has promoted some of it as an East Anglian farm ride. Nevertheless it comprises three parts, the riverside walk, the views from higher up the valley, and the stroll through the fine houses in Ford Street.

The Walk

From the Shoulder of Mutton cross the river Colne by the A604 road bridge. As you look over the bridge to the right you will see first the river and then the millrace bypass flowing east towards Colchester. The river here is the boundary between Fordham and Aldham. At Bridge House turn right by an old green wooden public footpath sign marked 'footpath to Chappel'. It also bears the logo of the Essex Way – an 81 mile long distance way from Epping to Harwich. We are walking part of it westwards along a twitten between a brick wall and a wooden fence. Shortly you continue between a wooden fence and a hedge. Cross a fine railed bridge and bear right down to the riverside.

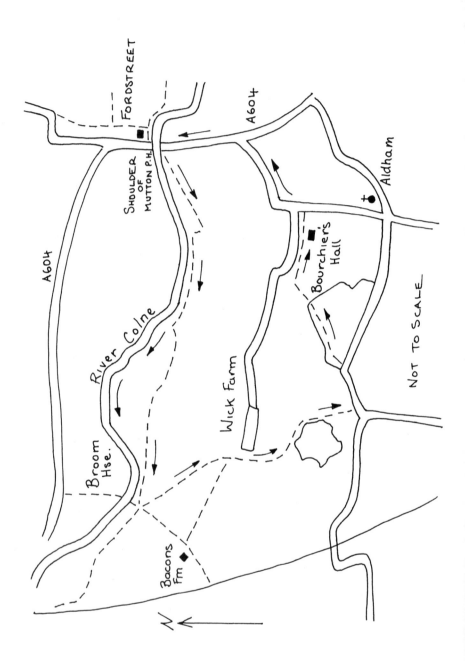

FORDSTREET

A604

Aldham

SHOULDER OF MUTTON P.H.

A604

River Colne

Bourchiers' Hall

Broom Hse.

Wick Farm

NOT TO SCALE

Bacons Fm

N

Turn left along the river bank. There is a large nursery on your left. You cross over a boat mooring point by way of another substantial bridge and leave the nursery behind, coming to an arable field. Follow a good headland path past a Second World War defence installation. How many of these were built in Essex, never to be used? Follow the wide track away from the river and then gradually back. Finally, after a left and right bend you reach a new wooden bridge and stile. The stile is sited quite near the river so be careful not to jump off the stile into the water! Now you are in the pasture lands of the sheep of Bacons Farm. Walk on along the bank till you reach a brick bridge. On your right is Broom House – a pink building. Turn back on your line and head south east past a solitary tree making for a substantial metal railed, concrete bridge in the hedge. Look back for the railway viaduct at Chappel and to its left Popes Hall. The whole view of the Colne valley from here is one of the best views in inland Essex.

Cross the bridge and turn right on a wide headland. At the field corner turn left, climbing and later turning to right and left to reach a stretch of woodland near Wick Farm. At a series of arrows pointing to the right, a permissive footpath goes round two sides of the next field leading up a slope with the woods on your right. At the corner turn right along the eastern edge of the woods, finally following an arrow out to a crossroads. Turn left, signposted to Aldham. Ahead is the Aldham church spire.

When you reach a stile and a concrete footpath sign turn left over the stile and follow the crop division to the field boundary. Turn right and follow the ditch and hedge on your left. Go through the gap in the facing hedge and turn left and right through the pedestrian access. Continue on a broad track with a hedge on your right and a fence on your left past the agricultural buildings. The track is now pebble based with the hedge on your left and the fence on your right. Do not be deterred by the notice of a guard dog patrol. The farm road now swings to the right and you continue past an attractive farmhouse and over a stile. Here on your right is the sight of Bourchier's Hall, an unusual white building. Go downhill to reach the road, turning left when you get there and follow on down to Ford Street passing Mill Race Nursery and Fore Acres – a fine timbered building.

Turn left along Ford Street. There are several nice houses including two more pubs! The Coopers Arms on the west side and the Queens Head on the east side. Most imposing is Old House, now a bed and breakfast establishment, but many hundreds of years old. Cross back over the river and look for the double house at the mill, one brick and one timbered.

Fuller Street
The Square and Compasses

Fuller Street derives from Fullwood Street or Folewode (14th century) meaning foul, dirty wood! If it was so, the wood in question must have been felled long ago, for the several woods hereabouts are anything but foul or dirty. Fuller Street just about scrapes up enough houses to be called a village. It belongs to the Fairstead parish – that village being even smaller. The Square and Compasses is a friendly pub, for visitors are not so many that they are not welcomed by the 'locals' for a conversation. In winter, the opening hours are Monday to Saturday 12 noon-3 pm and 7 pm-11 pm; in summer 11.30 am-3 pm and 6.30 pm-11 pm. On Sunday, it is open throughout the year from 12 noon-3 pm and 7 pm-10.30 pm. Traditional pub meals and bar snacks are available.

The Square and Compasses is a tenancy from Ridleys Breweries, so it is not surprising that Ridleys IPA Bitter is poured by gravity with normally an excellent result. Draught Strongbow cider is also

available. Children (and dogs) are allowed in with the proviso that they all behave themselves.
Telephone: 01245 361477.

How to get there: From the south leave the A12 at Hatfield Peverel and follow the signs to Terling. In Terling, Fuller Street is signed. From the A131 (Braintree – Chelmsford) turn to the east at Great Leighs (St. Anne's Castle pub) and again look for the signs to Fuller Street.

Parking: The parking space is fairly generous but please ask before you leave for your walk.

Length of the walk: 4¾ miles. OS Map Landranger series 167, Chelmsford and Harlow (GR 748161).

The epithet 'back in time' is suitable for this walk, passing as it does two lovely woods on the slopes of the rolling Ter valley and the sights of attractive Terling coming between the charm of Fairstead and Fuller Street.

The Walk

From the pub walk down to the road. This walk has an old world feel about it, and Fuller Street, which is a collection of houses passed by the Essex Way, is no exception. Turn to your left and follow the street round for 250 yards until you come to a footpath sign on your right. Follow this path past the side of a house and garden and along the edge of a field to the field corner. Turn right through the hedge and a few yards further on turn left down to a bridge. Cross over the river Ter and walk up a hill to the edge of a large wood (Sandy Wood). Follow the wood all the way up and turn left along a good track, still with the wood on your left. At the far corner of the wood turn left and shortly right to a second corner of the wood. Now walk across the field going east towards a stile on the other side. Cross this to enter the village of Terling.

Terling is the seat of the Rayleighs and is undoubtedly one of the most attractive villages in Essex. Terling Place occupies a magnificent park of 200 acres. Henry VIII had a palace here. Both have gone long since. In the nearby churchyard is a small monument of red sandstone. It is the grave of John William Strutt, the third Lord Rayleigh and one of the most learned men who ever lived in England. He died at the end of the First World War and such was his contribution to scientific discovery that he received the Nobel Prize, the Order of Merit, and academic honours. From entering Terling walk up past various cottages passing a pond and turning left along the Waltham Road. Take

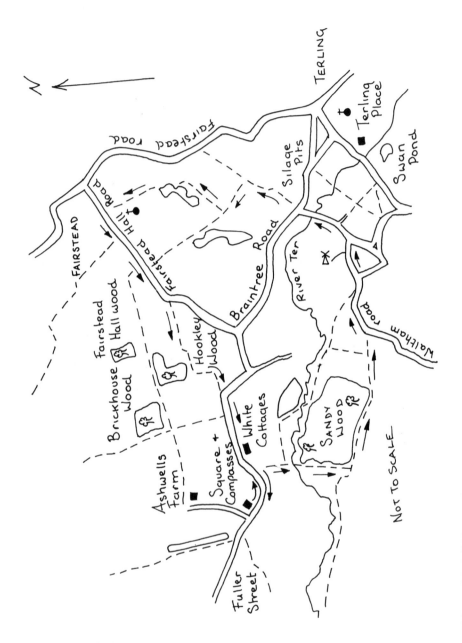

40

the left fork (Hull Road) and shortly, at the next road on the left, you will spot the windmill, looking spic and span. It is now a private residence. Continuing downhill, you will reach the river again but this time the cars can cross only by driving through a large splash. Walkers may do likewise but there is a drier route for them over a pedestrian bridge. Carry on up to a road, where the route turns left. If you want to visit the church, Terling Place or the pub turn right.

To continue the walk turn left for a few yards to a footpath sign. Walk up this field past some silage pits and then with a hedge on your right. At the top corner of the field where a pond is visible by the hedge, turn left and walk down this field edge with the hedge on your right. To your left is a fine view of the windmill. At the end of the field, turn right over the shallow ditch and go through a gate with an earth bridge into the next field. Turn right by the waymark and walk (northeast) with a hedge on your right. Forty yards from the end of this field turn left across the field and follow the waymarks through the wood. Now turn right along the field edge. Turn left along a narrow grass strip towards Fairstead church. On the way cross two stiles and a plank bridge to reach a road (Fairstead Hall Road).

In a village as remote as any in Essex, with a tiny population, Fairstead church boasts Roman bricks, wall paintings over 700 years old, and a 600 years old bell in the belfry. Just to sit in front of the church is a solace in itself. From here turn left and walk along the road. Take the third footpath sign at a corner of the road and walk to Hookley Wood, passing along the southern edge. When it ends turn left and walk south for 200 yards then turn right across the field back to the road. Now follow the road (west) past a row of cottages (White Cottages) and retrace your steps back to your car at the Square and Compasses.

Fyfield
The Black Bull

Fyfield (meaning 'five hides' of land) has won high praise in the past. Here we shall find ourselves in a lovable old place where life can have changed very little since Elizabethan times. The country is as gentle and dreamy as any that a lover of England could hope or wish to find. The Black Bull has been presiding over all this for 600 years, though not with precisely the same building. A little remodelling inside has made the pub more spacious, but the internal wall with its lovely wood panelling remains throughout.

Opening hours are 11 am-2.30 pm and 6.30 pm-11 pm, Mondays to Saturdays, 12 noon-3 pm and 7 pm-10.30 pm on Sundays. Meals may be had between the hours 12 noon-1.45 pm and 7 pm-9.30 pm throughout the week. A wide range of home-made food is available, with chilli and curry dishes something of a speciality. The Black Bull is a freehouse with two real ales on draught, Courage Bitter and Directors. Dry Blackthorn cider is on tap. Children are welcome, but are expected to behave. O yes, I am assured that a lady ghost is in residence, but fear not, she has never been seen outside the owners' rooms.

Telephone: 01277 899225.

How to get there: Turn off north from the Four Wantz roundabout at Chipping Ongar on the A414. The road is the B184 and Fyfield is about 2 miles from the roundabout.

Parking: At the pub. You may leave your car while you walk, but please ask before you do so.

Length of the walk: 3 miles. OS Map Landranger series 167 Chelmsford and Harlow (GR 572072).

I find this route among the best of its kind. Pretty pretty it may not be, but for an hour's demonstration of unspoilt rural beauty it is very high on the list. There are wild areas, animals, river crossings and plenty more to look at. When you reach the church try a 200 yard diversion to the left to view the river before reaching the old mill.

The Walk

Coming out of the pub, cross the road and walk up the lane almost opposite, signposted 'to Norwood End only'. It is slightly to your right. Go past a footpath sign on your left. When the lane soon turns off to the right, carry straight on up a green track. When you finally come to an open field in front of you turn left (south) across a field to a sign 'please keep dogs on lead'. Here you are walking through set aside land which may become a nature reserve. Follow the path through this rough area to cross a wooden bridge (rather hidden behind a willow tree) over a stream. Now turn right along a wire fence and cross a bridge and stile over the fence (another demand is made here for the restraint of dogs). The walking surface is now smooth. You turn half right and walk towards a gap near a fence. Go through this with the fence on your right and cross a stile into a field where cattle graze. Continue on for a few yards to a stile in the right hand fence. Cross this and turn left along a farm track to a road. On your left is The Gypsy Meads restaurant, scene of many a Sunday afternoon tea in the 50s and 60s.

You are now in the little area known as Clatterford End, and you continue walking south to the footpath sign pointing to your left. Here, cross a quite busy road and walk to the left of a garage and past a house to a stile. Cross the stile and continue on the edge of a field till you reach playing fields and the village on your left. Bear right and follow the hedge on your left for the length of the playing fields,

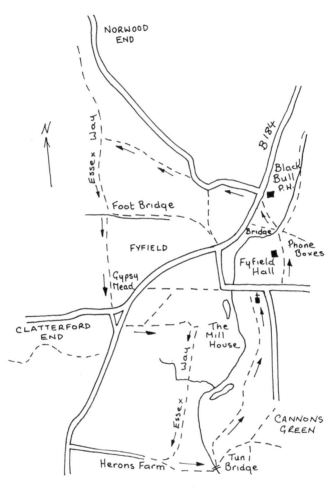

NOT TO SCALE

finally passing to right and left round a clump of bushes. Now turn right and follow a good grass track with a fence on your right to a plank bridge crossing a stream. Having done this go straight over a large field to reach what used to be called a RUPP. These were old roads no longer open to traffic but used as paths. You get in to the middle of this, turn left and walk downhill (east) as far as you can. The RUPP leads down to the river but is often very boggy at the bottom so there is an escape route on the right to walk along the field edge. You will arrive at the Tun Bridge and cross over the Roding. This is a peaceful spot. On a sunny day try looking for fish, birds, and butterflies. Yes, the Roding is at its best around Fyfield.

After crossing the bridge take the path on the left going north up the river. Later you pass a reservoir, then the backs of houses to reach the church, which is reputedly the most extraordinary village church in Essex. It looks as if it was a series of afterthoughts. Perhaps it was. The interior, however, is most impressive with a splendid chancel and a lavish set of three sedilia.

At the road turn right from the church and after a few yards turn left at a footpath sign to walk north past a graveyard of mechanical things and phone boxes. Now turn left to a bridge over the river. At this point there are actually footpaths in five directions, but if you look over to your right (north west) you will probably recognise the Black Bull, and you can make your way over these meadows towards it. Finally there is a stile into the pub car park.

Goldhanger
The Chequers

The Chequers and Goldhanger have a long history together. It is well known that in the days when smuggling was a frequent occupation all along the Blackwater estuary, Goldhanger played a leading part. Clearly the Chequers must have been the meeting ground for many a deal. Also when Osea Island was a home for curing alcoholics it is thought that bootleg liquor from the Chequers found its way by rowing boat to the island's patients! Strange that when the Chequers was first opened in 1410 it was in fact a courthouse. Becoming a coaching inn in 1560, its most famous guest was the Tsar of Russia. To this day it still does bed and breakfast.

There is a wide selection of food, bar snacks, bar meals and a restaurant. Opening hours at the bar are 11 am-2.30 pm and 6.30 pm-11 pm, Mondays to Saturdays, 12 noon-3 pm and 7 pm-10.30 pm on Sundays. Food is served till ½ hour before the end of each session. Everything is home-made and served with fresh vegetables. Obviously scampi is frozen but go on Fridays for lovely fresh, locally caught fish.

Real ales currently available are Greene King IPA, Tolly Cobbold, and Burton Ale. For cider try Dry Blackthorn. Children are welcome and dogs, providing they all behave. There is a sheltered garden at the rear.

Telephone: 01621 788203.

How to get there: Goldhanger is on the B1026 from Heybridge near Maldon. The Chequers is next to the church in the middle of the village.

Parking: The pub has a car park opposite on the other side of the road (please mention that you are leaving your car there before you walk). Otherwise street parking is possible near the church.

Length of the walk: 5½ miles. OS Map Landranger series 168 Colchester and the Blackwater (GR 905087).

A fine walk giving first, on the way to Chappel Farm and Rook Hall, the distant perspective of the delightful village you have left. The permissive path through Chigborough fisheries provides the calm of lakeside followed by the many pleasures of the sea wall back to Goldhanger. The tide may be in or out. It may be windy. The birds, the causeway. All this and the possibility of an ice cream!

The Walk

On leaving the pub investigate the old village pump – children will be especially interested in working out where the water comes out. The walk proceeds along Head Street. There is an interesting gate at Hatters Lodge. Don't miss the intriguing planning of cottages 5/7. How many of us can boast an 1839 Wesleyan chapel at the bottom of the garden? But enough of sight seeing, let's get on with the walk.

Continue west to the junction of Head Street and Maldon Road. Here a footpath sign indicates the route ahead on a field edge beside the allotments so carefully tended all the year round. The field path continues first to the left of the gardens to some recently reroofed cottages and the road called Blind Lane at a new black footpath sign marked 4. Turn left and stop after a few yards to admire the wide open views all round, also the flowers and bullrushes in the banks of this narrow road.

At a footpath sign marked 2 take a westerly bearing towards and to the right of the whitewashed cottage at Chappel Farm. Cross a new plank bridge and head for the gap in the hedge which, as you will see when you get nearer, is marked with a yellow arrow. Cross the field on a visible path to a new plank bridge. Continue ahead and look for

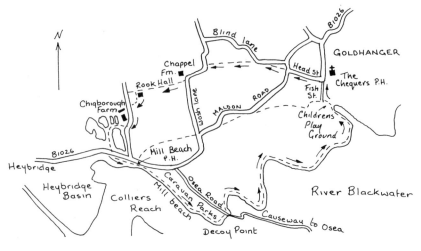

the signpost straight ahead in Wash Lane. Turn left but do glance back to see the pretty village of Goldhanger and note how the church appears to be keeping watch over the homes standing near it. Continue down the lane, stopping to greet the Chappel Farm dog who likes to chat with passing walkers. Pass the thatched cottage on your left, cross a stream and turn right at a footpath signpost. Follow the field edge with the ditch on your right. At the cross track by the hedge gap, keep straight ahead until you reach the farm buildings of Rook Hall ahead. When you reach the farm head for the track beside the barn. Some 50 paces on, turn left on a wider farm track to pass Rook Hall farmhouse on your left. Note the fine collection of evergreen trees in the garden as you go down the drive. Pass a yellow brick bungalow and two farmworkers' cottages as you make your way out to Chigborough Road. Turn left and walk south down the road passing the sprawling Chigborough Lodge on your right. Note its unusual wrought iron chimney mounts.

Enter Chigborough fisheries, ignoring the red 'no entry' signs and pass the SAGA sign on the right. Follow the track as it leads you right then left around the end of the first lake, where fishermen are busy on their boats or on the bank whenever the weather is good enough. As you continue round the lake the path rises and you pass a series of ponds to take the first small path right on a willow lined track just past the last pond on your right, and to the left of a gate. At the first crossing track turn right for 24 paces on a courtesy path, then left again onto a good grass track with a second large lake on your right. Pass the fishermen's car park and the road at a footpath post marked

29. Turn left and take great care on the busy road passing Bridge Bungalow, Chigborough Road and the Hall Aggregates site.

On reaching Mill Beach pub turn right and walk through the car park to the left of the building to reach the sea wall. Here take in the good views of Heybridge and Northey Island. Turn left to pass the caravan site. There is a shop where ice cream can be purchased, or try the nearby Osea stores and coffee shop. Continue ahead noting Osea Island and Goldhanger Creek. Later at Decoy Point pass the causeway which links the island to the mainland at low tide.

The distant church of Goldhanger begins to beckon you on a long game of hide and seek as it appears and disappears behind nearby trees. Along the sea wall Bradwell power station appears on the far bank of the river Blackwater. Pass by a track marked 'No Path Private'. Perhaps this stretch of wall is a good place for a short rest to watch the seabirds and enjoy the otherwise peaceful beauty. Pass the Goldhanger Sailing Club as you head inland to cross the stile at the end of the creek. At the next bend in the sea wall path take the steps down to the sloe-lined gravel path, passing the children's playing fields to a footpath sign marked 13. Turn right into Fish Street. Note the lack of thatch at Thatch End. Children may count the fish on the houses including the large blue fish at the sea wall and the brown fish at number 2. Look for the observatory that towers over one of the roofs. In no time you reach the Chequers and your car.

Great Tey
The Chequers

St. Barnabas church has an early Norman crossing tower, regarded as among the finest pieces of Norman architecture in the county. The building declares to us that we are approaching somewhere that was a centre of busy life ages ago. It would be nice to know the reasons for this display in this location. Many Roman bricks are in the walls and arches and about the village and at nearby farms are 15th, 16th and 17th century houses and cottages. Sadly the Norman nave and aisles of the church were pulled down this century. It was, wrongly, thought to be cheaper to pull it down than to rebuild. We must be thankful for those nice things that were preserved.

The pub has been standing near the church for about 400 years – it was originally a merchant's house. There are also records of another inn and a small brewery nearby. Food is available all week, 12 noon-2 pm and 7 pm-9.30 pm, Sundays 12 noon-2 pm and 6.30 pm-9.30 pm. A roast meal is served at Sunday lunch times and almost all the food is home-made. Hearty favourites include beef in beer casserole and pork goulash Hungarian.

The Chequers is one of a number of Greene King pubs in the north of Essex. Opening times are 11 am-3 pm and 6.30 pm-11 pm on Mondays to Saturdays, 12 noon-3 pm and 7 pm-10.30 pm on Sundays, and the real ales served are IPA and Abbott, but, as the landlord says, due to the distance from the bar to the cellar it is necessary to have a very small amount of top pressure. Taunton Blackthorn is the cider on tap. At the rear and side of the pub there is a very fine old walled garden, and families can drink there – children are welcome to eat indoors. Reasonably behaved dogs are also welcome.

Telephone: 01206 210814.

How to get there: The most direct route to Great Tey whether coming from the west or the east of the county is by the A120 between Coggeshall and Marks Tey. A minor road goes north to Great Tey and Wakes Colne from a mile or so west of Marks Tey. Take the left turn off this at Great Tey church and the Chequers is just behind.

Parking: Parking is available at the pub, and it should be fine to leave your car there, but please ask at the bar before setting out on the walk. The pub is in a quiet street so street parking is also available.

Length of the walk: 2 ½ miles. OS Map Landranger series 168 Colchester and the Blackwater (GR 891258).

A short walk in a parish where life seems peaceful and taken at a modest pace. The thatched barn at Teybrook Farm is worth inspection, as is Chase Cottage, but most of your sight seeing will be at the church.

The Walk

Turn right outside the Chequers and right down the side of the building. Entering the churchyard, even the most enthusiastic walker is slightly reluctant to pass by this magnificent tower, but that is what you must eventually do. Follow the path through the yard out to Brook Road, leading to the Tey brook which we will encounter later. Tey brook is the name given to the upper waters of the Roman river rising near Great Tey which runs into the river Colne at Rowhedge. Hence Great Tey, Little Tey, and Marks Tey. It is thought that sometimes rivers change their names with the influence of powerful people down river.

Turn right down Brook Road past a nice looking house named 'The Barn'. The next property is the Rectory with a large moated garden as perhaps befits the huge church tower opposite. Turn left at a concrete footpath post and follow a good headland path with the hedge and

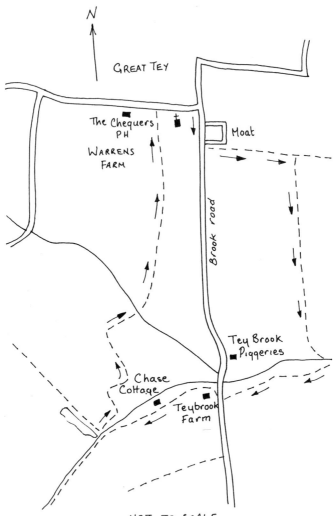

N

GREAT TEY

The Chequers
PH

WARRENS
FARM

Moat

Brook road

Tey Brook
Piggeries

Chase
Cottage

Teybrook
Farm

NOT TO SCALE

moat on your left. When the moat turns away from the path continue
with the field edge. After walking in all 400 yards from the road, turn
right (south) across the field. Look for and walk towards a solitary tree
about 200 yards distant. There is in fact a line of four trees leading you
towards the left edge of a small group of tall trees by the brook, at the
far end of the field. Between the end of these and a willow tree leaning
over there is a bridge made of old railway sleepers which enables you

to cross the brook. Turn right behind the group of trees and follow a good farm track (west) to Teybrook Farm.

You approach the road by a concrete footpath post and a magnificent old thatched barn. Turn right for a few yards and left across the road to another footpath post, by a white fence. Here there are four logs to enable you to cross the fence and walk along the side of a corrugated shed on your left. Cross a track and keep up the hill to enter a field with a fence on your right. Now walk on past the delightful Chase Cottage (thatched) and a pond. Continue over a field to a railed bridge in the corner which crosses a stream. The bridge was sited here years ago after a lot of persuasion by the Ramblers' Association in Essex, and, whilst it slopes somewhat, it is nice to see that it stands up to the traffic of many pairs of boots each year from those travelling on the Essex Way. We now follow this route into Great Tey.

Turn right along the stream, then left away from it. Now again turn right. At the corner, though the map shows the path to the left on the east side of the fence, you are asked to walk on the west side with a ditch on your right. At the corner turn right again. When the hedge ends, continue 50 yards across the field to a bridge near a water treatment plant. The path goes between a hedge and the treatment plant out to an open field. Follow the edge of the field with a ditch on your left. The church tower has been growing all the way from Teybrook Farm and it now assumes dominating proportions, ie it towers! Cross a concrete driveway at the end of the field and make your way through bushes to the field in front of the church. Keep to the left of this field to go through a gate and past some cottages to the Chequers.

Helions Bumpstead
The Three Horseshoes

The name Bumpstead is shared with Steeple Bumpstead, and is believed to mean 'a place where reeds grow'. Helions derives from Tihel the Breton who held the manor in 1086 as quoted in Domesday Book, from Helléan in Morbihan, Brittany. St. Andrew's church stands proudly over the village, positioned some way up (you've guessed it) Church Hill. Parts of it date back to the 13th century, notably the chancel and arch. The old woodwork, benches, chancel seats, and pews are the main features in this village church. Sadly the tower collapsed in 1812, and was replaced by a red brick one, which, nevertheless, blends nicely with the more ancient parts.

Somewhat older than the church tower are parts of the Three Horseshoes, which are in fact 17th century. It is a true village local about 2 miles from its nearest rival. It is a good example of a Greene King tenancy, where pride is taken in keeping the beer and preparing the food, and the vast majority of the customers are regulars well known to the landlord. You will be made welcome and not only because in these fairly remote parts of Essex a stranger can be a source of information or gossip! Opening times are 11.45 am-2.30 pm and 7 pm-11 pm on Monday to Saturdays, 12 noon-2.30 pm and 7 pm-10.30 pm on Sundays. Food is available till 2 pm on Mondays to Saturdays and from 7 pm-10 pm on Wednesday to Saturday evenings. There is a good menu – of mainly home-made food, with specials which are changed regularly. At lunchtimes you can enjoy the good old 'pub grub' favourites – ploughman's lunches, sausage, egg and chips and juicy gammon steaks.

Real ales are Greene King IPA and Abbott Ale, both served by handpump, and the draught cider is Taunton Blackthorn. Children are welcomed in to eat with their parents, and dogs are permitted in the Village bar, provided they behave. The garden at the rear has been enlarged, and can be an enchanting place in which to eat and drink, sheltered by the hill from the west. We think you will want to bring your friends here for a return visit.

Telephone: 01440 730298.

How to get there: From the south, east, or west, the desired route is towards Steeple Bumpstead. From Saffron Walden there is a signposted turn off the B1054 before reaching Steeple Bumpstead up Water Lane to Helions Bumpstead. From Great Dunmow it's the B1057 all the way to Steeple Bumpstead, and from Colchester it's the A604, turning off left at New England on the B1054 to Steeple Bumpstead. From there work your way round this pretty village turning northwards off the B1054. The Three Horseshoes is near the church in Water Lane. I hope you can follow all that, but if in trouble ask the folks about these parts for clarification. They are friendly people!

Parking: The Three Horseshoes has quite an amount of parking space but please ask before setting out on your walk.

Length of the walk: 3½ miles. OS Map Landranger series 154 Cambridge and Newmarket (GR 650415).

Walking in three counties in the space of an hour and a half is not an every day experience. Most of this route is on firm tracks, lanes and roads, so it can be confidently attempted in all seasons. There are fine wide views over this northerly part of Essex, as well as of parts of Suffolk and Cambridgeshire, all for the effort invested in a gentle climb of 100 ft.

The Walk

The lowest point in Helions Bumpstead is 289 ft – well above the Essex average, yet the village seems to nestle amongst its surrounding landscape. Moreover, as we shall see, the adjoining counties of Cambridgeshire and Suffolk are not much more than a mile distant – closer than the nearest village in Essex – Steeple Bumpstead. Turn left along Water Lane when you leave the Three Horseshoes. At the crossroads turn left up Sages End Lane, soon walking out of the village past Rolls Farm to a road corner. The farm here is Sage's End and the name stems from Geoffrey Le Sage in the 13th century. Turn right at

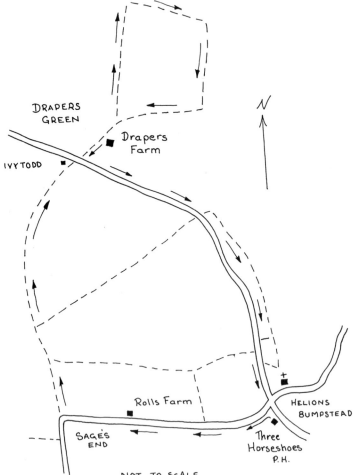

a concrete bridleway sign numbered 59 and walk up a good grass track. At the top of the little hill the track turns to the right and the way becomes concrete. Shortly there is a bench on the left from where views may be enjoyed of Helions church and beyond to the south east.

Continue on to reach the Bartlow Road at Drapers Green by a concrete bridleway sign and a post box. Cross the road turning right, and turn left down Drapers Lane, prettily set on the right with bushes and young trees. As you come to Draper's Farm a concrete bridleway sign points through the steading which you follow. The name Draper also dates back to the 13th century. Continue up a wide green lane. The lane is 'double ditched' for 600 yards until you reach a solitary tree on the right. From here the path follows the ditch on the left to an old wooden bridge with new metal hand rails. At this point take stock. The field over the ditch on the left is in Cambridgeshire, while ahead across the bridge lies Suffolk. If the famous Jake the Peg with his extra leg had been with us here, he could simultaneously have had a foot in each of the three counties!

Cross the bridge into Suffolk and turn right along the headland path. After 200 yards cross a shallow ditch into the next field. Come to a bush and turn right over an earth bridge back into Essex. Now follow a good track south for 450 yards. When the track turns right by a tree stump follow it and after a further 400 yards rejoin the wide lane you walked up previously. Turn left and retrace your steps through Draper's Farm up Drapers Lane to Bartlow Road. Turn left to walk down this road. It is a fairly quiet road but there is little in the way of a pathway or verge, so keep in to the right facing any oncoming traffic.

On the way down the road into Helions Bumpstead village there are some really old buildings interspersed with some of a much more recent vintage. I feel the combination works better sometimes than others. Near the church there are 'Pilgrims Waye' and 'Moss's Farmhouse' on the right, and 'The Old Marquis' on the left. Thus you return to the heart of the village to rejoin your car at the Three Horseshoes.

Horndon On The Hill
The Bell Inn

The village has a wealth of history having been a centre for trade situated on the main route from East Anglia to Kent and the channel ports. Ferries across the Thames at Tilbury probably date back to Roman times. Horndon rose to a position of considerable social and commercial importance during the 14th and 15th centuries. The Bell, an impressive building, half timbered with gables, was constructed in the 15th century. From early days it was a coaching inn, as can be seen from the courtyard. Coaches would come and go through the archway carrying farmers and other travellers to and from London, and the hay and corn markets. At least one 'burning at the stake' was carried out at the back of the Bell. Thomas Highbed, a farmer, was charged and condemned of heresy in 1555. A fire was prepared and Thomas, a local hero, walked into it having addressed his judges. The Bell has recently become a freehouse and has been in the same family since 1938.

Opening times are 11 am-2.30 pm and 6 pm-11 pm on Mondays to Saturdays, 12 noon-3 pm and 7 pm-10.30 pm on Sundays. Food is served every day till 2 pm in the afternoon and 10 pm in the evening.

On offer is imaginative English and international cooking with the full menu, which changes daily, available both in the restaurant and the bar. When I was there the lamb cutlets in pastry with rosemary mousse appealed to my taste buds – it was a difficult choice to make between that and the chicken casserole and beef and vegetable stew. Real ales are Charrington IPA and Bass, with a third which is varied, and Taunton Blackthorn cider is also on tap.

Telephone: 01375 642463.

How to get there: With the new bypass arrangement Horndon village can only be approached from the north side, either by way of the A13 or from the A127 by the B1007 from Dunton or the B1036 from Basildon. Drive up the High Road and just before going downhill again the Bell is on the left. Don't attempt to go in by the entrance from coaching days – the car park entrance is well marked.

Parking: The Bell car park is sizeable and will probably accommodate your car providing you ask at the bar before setting off for your walk. Otherwise street parking is available.

Length of the walk: 3 miles. OS Map Landranger series 178 The Thames Estuary (GR 671833).

A short walk down the hill where sheep grazed on the Thames flood plain. The climb back up goes by Arden Hall where Queen Elizabeth stayed after reviewing the Armada troops at Tilbury.

The Walk

Starting a walk from the top of a hill has the inevitable consequence that it is nicely downhill at the start but of course uphill at the finish! As the differential in this case is barely 100 ft and the views afforded from the start and middle of the walk are high, wide, and handsome by way of compensation, no sleep need be lost. Leave the Bell and turn right to find at the end of the building a footpath sign, 'To Stanford Le Hope'. The path finds its way narrowly between a fence on the left and the inn on the right. At the end of the building continue downhill eastwards with a hedge on your left.

At the bypass road a stile by a footpath sign and steps bear you up to the road. Cross over to another footpath sign and stile. Continue on your eastward line with a hedge on your left. When the hedge ends a good path has been left in, leading to a small wood. Enter the wood and turn right with a stream on your left. After 20 yards find a bridge. At present this is in poor repair but is reasonably secure with the help of the handrail. Cross the stream. Now cross the field to the east

59

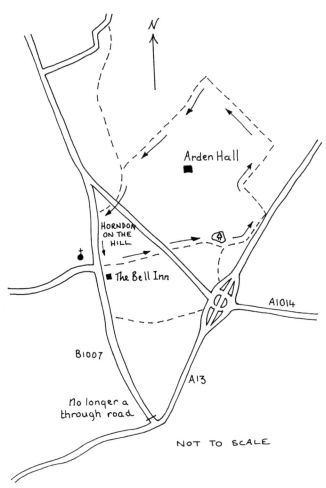

N

Arden Hall

HORNDON
ON THE
HILL

The Bell Inn

A1014

B1007

A13

No longer a
through road

NOT TO SCALE

towards the A13 where two footpath signs beckon. Turn left for 250 yards along the fence to come to another footpath sign. Cross a stile and turn left (north west) up a farm track for 400 yards to a facing hedge at a footpath sign.

Turn right along a good headland path with the hedge on your left. When you spot a pond on your right turn left through a gap, climbing towards a thicket ahead with first a hedge and ditch on your right and then across an open field. Enter the thicket and walk through it past a badger sett and find a stile on your left which you cross. Walk across the field to a gap and stile by a stream. Walk now with the hedge on your left. When the stream turns south away from the hedge, cross a stile to the other side of the hedge, and continue south west to a further stile. This one was in need of renewal when I was last there. Now walk slightly left to a bridge and stile in the facing hedge and through to a field by Wrens Park Farm on your right and Arden Hall on your left. Walk half left to the opposite corner of this field at a bridge and stile. From here walk almost due south to another stile and then diagonally right to a stile and footpath sign at the bypass. Cross the bypass with care and from a footpath sign and stile continue uphill across a little field to a track which leads up to the corner of North Hill and Hillcrest Road. Look back at Arden Hall, one of the more considerable manors in Horndon in Georgian times.

Now walk up Horndon High Road. There are allotments on the left, and an old school on the right, with its replacement behind it. Two thatched cottages shelter among much younger neighbours. Halls Row cottages are interesting but undated. The Woolmarket was erected in the 1500s. It was here that the Dutch merchants who had moored their vessels at nearby Mucking or Fobbing came to trade in the wool from the sheep grazing below the village. The building now serves as a meeting place for the villagers. A short detour along Orsett Road on the right will take you to the church of St. Peter and St. Paul, with its avenue of lime trees up to the porch. Largely Early English of the 13th century, it has a splendid 15th century chancel roof and a simply beautiful font, a rare design. The Bell is beyond the Woolmarket on the left.

Little Baddow
The Rodney

The Rodney is an 18th century building. In the late 1840s Charles Smith was in residence here as a baker, grocer, and beerseller, so it was natural when The Old Rodney in the Warren up the hill became a private dwelling that Charles should move the sign to his establishment. The pub is accustomed to walkers calling in and excellent home-cooked food is provided. Indeed it is often as well to make a reservation. Families with young children can be served in the back lounge. There is a pleasant beer garden, and if you prefer you may just buy drinks and eat your own sandwiches in the garden.

Currently Greene King IPA and Rayments Special real ales are on offer, and also Dry Blackthorn cider. The hours for eating are 12 noon-2 pm and 7 pm-9 pm Monday to Saturday and 12 noon-9 pm on Sunday. The bar hours are 11.30 am-2.30 pm and 7 pm-11 pm Monday to Saturday and 12 noon-10.30 pm on Sunday.

Telephone: 01245 222385.

How to get there: Little Baddow is east of Chelmsford and about 3 miles from Boreham village. From Boreham church follow Church Road to the east and south to cross the river Chelmer. At the road junction turn left and pass Little Baddow church and Holybreds Farm. At the T junction turn right for a few yards up North Hill to the Rodney.

Parking: At the pub. Please ask permission to leave your car before setting out on your walk.

Length of the walk: 3½ miles. OS Map Landranger series 167 Chelmsford and Harlow (GR 779079).

A magnificent walk round the nature reserves and Woodham Walter Common to the east of Little Baddow village. Like most hilly walks we start uphill and climb through Heather Hills. Postmans Lane leads to a footpath crossroads marked by a multi bridleway signpost. Then we go through Woodham Walter Common to emerge from the woods at Spring Elms and downhill across a field to Bassetts before 'westering' home through Bassetts Wood and Warren Farm to the Rodney.

The Walk

Leaving the pub turn right uphill. After 250 yards a footpath sign on the left indicates a path which gradually leaves the road (south easterly). Here you are in an area known as Heather Hills (between Scrub Wood and the Warren), a 16 acre section of scrub wood. It once belonged to Lord Raleigh, but was bought in the early 1920s by Mr. and Mrs. Gregory Nicholson of Dukes Orchard who presented Heather Hills to the village so that it should be open to the public for all time. 'The bramble and bracken, the steep slopes, the wide view, the heather, the seclusion, the liberty to wander that the place offers, make it a favourite playground' wrote Reverend Jesse Berridge in 1925. From the concrete footpath direction post follow the path straight on ignoring turn offs to the right. Having climbed for about 200 yards the path descends for a further 70 yards turning slightly right to a point where there is a wire fence on your left and a steep slope up on the right. Turn left uphill keeping the remains of the fence on your left till you reach a junction with a crossing bridleway. Turn right uphill and follow this to the Old Rodney House. You enter the grounds of the house by a Heather Hills notice through two gate posts. Past the house is a sunken tennis club. In past centuries this has been an alehouse, pleasure gardens, and a hotel restaurant. It had various names including The Warren House, The Cock and Warren, The Old Rodney, and the Old Rodney Hotel, advertising lunches, teas, and hard tennis courts. Of these only the tennis remains.

Tofts Chase

TOFTS

BASSETTS

To Boreham A12

Warren Farm

Bassetts Wood

The Rodney P.H.

LITTLE BADDOW

Old Rodney

SPRING ELMS

Colam la.

The Ridge

N

Birch Wood

Pheasant house Wood

Woodham Walter Common

To Danbury A414

Poors Piece

NOT TO SCALE

Continuing the walk take the left fork to reach a road. Here turn left for 130 yards to reach Postmans Lane on the right. Follow this (ignoring paths to left and right) for ½ mile or so to come to a signpost with four bridleway fingers pointing in all directions. You turn left (north east). After 300 yards the path veers left (into Woodham Walter Common) and 150 yards or so further on you keep to the right hand path, still walking north easterly. Keep on this track which is waymarked. A few yards before the garden of a house, turn left where blue arrows point left. Down the hill keep the wooden fence of the house garden in sight and when it becomes a wire fence the path

64

gets closer and at the bottom cross a bridge over a stream and go uphill to a road at Spring Elms.

Turn left along Spring Elms Lane for nearly 400 yards, looking out for a footpath sign on the right. Here a short green lane leads to a path across the field to a road at Bassetts, just within the Maldon district boundary. This house is believed to date back to about 1670. It was owned by Sir Mundeford Bramstone and assessed as six hearths for Hearth Tax! Just past the house a stile on the left leads to a path across a meadow (west). Find the stile entering Bassetts Wood and follow the path through (usually obvious but it can be a little overgrown). Exit the wood by a wooden bridge and stile. Continue up a short hill to cross over stiles in the fields south of Tofts. The 'walk in' to the pub consists of another footbridge and a series of stiles through Warren Farm. Here sheep do safely graze and we feel remote from civilization when suddenly the Rodney building emerges from below the path. I think you will wish to return again and again to Little Baddow – perhaps to repeat this walk or to explore further in this beautiful parish.

Littley Green
The Compasses Inn

Littley Green is a tiny hamlet some six miles from Chelmsford, Great Dunmow, or Braintree. It is in fact in the north east of Great Waltham parish and far away from the madding crowd. I see no shops, there is no church, but Littley Green boasts an excellent pub – the Compasses Inn, owned by Ridleys Brewery. Over the years I have often visited the Compasses in the course of rambling in the vicinity. I well remember the occasion a few years ago when one of my companions asked the landlord how long he had lived there. Sixty eight years was the answer, 'I came here with my father when I was eight!' After he retired the brewery made a few alterations but the beer is still poured by gravity in the cellar, six steps down from the bar. The real ales are Ridley IPA and Mild. There is a nice garden at the side and a children's room for rainy days. Dogs are welcome if reasonably behaved.

Opening hours are 11.30 am-3 pm and 6 pm-11 pm on Mondays to Saturdays, 12 noon-3 pm and 7 pm-10.30 pm on Sundays. Bar snacks are always available. The speciality is the Huffer, a large triangular roll which is an Essex baking feature and produced here with a variety of fillings.

How to get there: Coming from Chelmsford, go through Broomfield past the hospital. After the road bears right, turn left off it, signposted to Howe Street. At a point where the new road flies over, turn right under it and immediately left beside it. Both these turns are signposted to Littley Green which you reach in 1 ¼ miles. If you are travelling from Braintree, take the road round Little Waltham for the Howe Street turn off on the right, and proceed as above, at the point where the new road flies over.

Parking: There is good parking at the Compasses but please ask the landlord before you set out on your walk.

Length of the walk: 5 miles. OS Map Landranger series 167 Chelmsford and Harlow (GR 699172).

A grand trip round the Chelmer valley. The walk goes by several fine old houses, as well as passing part of Essex's beer heritage and traversing an ancient green lane.

The Walk
Leave the pub and turn right. Soon turn right again at a road signposted to Hartford End, and walk for 600 yards towards a group of houses and farm buildings. There are fine wide views to the left over the Chelmer valley. At Littleypark there is a beautiful old fashioned garden. Turn sharp left with the road and follow it as it drops downhill towards the river Chelmer. Just before reaching a crossing road you go into Uttlesford district. The industrial buildings ahead are in fact the source of pleasure to many – Ridleys brewery at Hartford End (the name Hartford signifies a crossing point for deer). For many years after Grays brewery closed in Chelmsford, Ridleys was the only brewery in Essex. It is still the only one with several retail houses. The Compasses at Littley Green is the nearest to the brewery and therefore earns the title of 'brewery tap'.

Turn left for a few yards and then at a concrete footpath sign turn right. Follow the drive to the mill house. This is the home of the Ridley family and it is one of those where the house is built over the river. Follow the drive over the river and past the house and continue through a gate. Turn left, and follow a path over a bridge crossing the secondary stream. Go through another metal gate and follow round the wood (The Gorse). When the wood ends, turn right up a field edge and follow the path south with the wood on your right. At the end

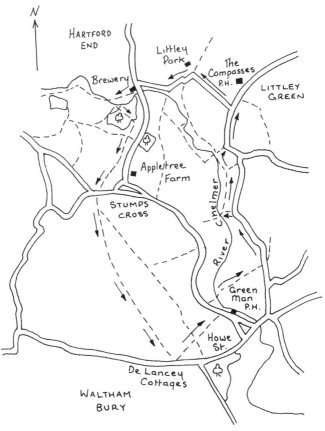

NOT TO SCALE

of the wood continue over a field to a crossing track. From here look back to the tranquil view of Littleypark across the valley.

Turn right and left to walk on a field edge with the hedge on your left. When the hedge ends continue across a field for 450 yards, aiming well to the left of a modern looking house. You reach a gap in the hedge ahead by a footpath sign. This is Stumps Cross where two roads, a path, and a green lane meet. Cross over the busy road and take the green lane (Dunmow Lane) to the left, running in glorious seclusion for 1¼ miles. Here in the spring you may find wild flowers to bring joy to your heart. When you reach nearly to the end of the lane, at Walthambury, turn left at a white topped footpath sign and you will see a tall white topped marker post on the ridge ahead. Walk across the field towards the post and continue with a ditch on your right to a second marker post. From here walk downhill aiming for a white building, The Green Man at Howe Street, thought to be the oldest pub in Essex.

Cross a stile into a small hilly pasture and then another stile out to the road. Turn left for 40 yards and then right at a concrete footpath sign. Go down the track and cross a stile by a gate and a farm bridge over the river Chelmer. Bear left across a meadow to a metal gate then over a rough field soon crossing two stiles on your right. Head uphill (east) with a hedge on your left to come to a road. This is the Essex Regiment Way, a bypass happily not too forbidding. Cross the road and soon come to a very fine building – Hill House. Turn left along the road, passing Barley Hill and Well House Farm.

After less than ½ mile come to Frogshall Cottage. A footpath sign points down a track to the left and you follow it, turning right along the field edge with the river on your left. Twenty yards before the hedge turns to your right, drop down to the left over a bridge and stile. Continue past a pond on your left to cross a stile then a bridge and stile. Near a bridge over the river there are three stiles. Cross the one to the right down steps to a sunken lane. Turn right and climb up to the green at Butlers, another fine old house. At a byway sign turn left along the road. Less than 250 yards further on you come back to Littley Green and the Compasses Inn is just through the village.

Manningtree
Manningtree Station Buffet

A pub with a difference! Just walk into the station (no ticket required) and turn right. In fact the buffet is a very early version of privatisation, having for 70 years been leased out by the railway authorities. The Real Ale Campaign encouraged those in charge to keep a selection of beers on handpump. Today this comprises Adnams Bitter, Adnams Broadside, Courage Directors, Marston's Pedigree, Mitchells Bitter, and Mauldons Black Adder. There is also available Strongbow cider on tap.

Here you can stoke up with some warming chilli con carne, steak and kidney pie or perhaps a good hot curry! A wide selection of home prepared food is available both in the buffet bar and in the restaurant adjoining, and children are made welcome. Be prepared for a friendly reception by the staff and other guests. Walkers are frequent visitors due to the proximity of the open countryside. We actually discovered the Buffet after completing a group ramble in the area about nine years ago, and have ever since made a point of visiting when in that part of the county. There is even an outdoor patio taken over from the station platform! Truly worth a visit.

The Buffet actually opens at 6 am, but only for food and non-alcoholic drinks till 10.30 am. It is then licensed all day till 11 pm. On Sunday, it is open 12 noon-3 pm and 7 pm-10.30 pm.

Telephone: 01206 391114.

How to get there: Leave the A12 at the junction with the A120. At the roundabout look carefully for signs to Ardleigh, and take the Ardleigh road which turns left immediately after the roundabout. Follow this minor road until it joins the A137 in Ardleigh. At Lawford this road turns left downhill to a roundabout. The first exit goes left to Manningtree station.

Parking: Station parking is officially free on Saturdays and Sundays. Monday to Friday Buffet customers are permitted to park along the side adjacent to the Buffet.

Length of the walk: 4 miles. OS Map Landranger series 168 Colchester and the Blackwater (GR 094322).

Like most towns that stand on a river, Manningtree is touched by the movements and reflections of the water to be made the more romantic. This walk in such a short space encompasses the beauty of the riverside, one of Constable's most famous subjects, the views from the elevation of Lawford church, together with the uniquely welcoming atmosphere of the Station Buffet. Need I say more?

The Walk

Below the station entrance there is a good wide walking track on which you travel west for about 600 yards before turning right under the railway. In another 350 yards the track turns left and you continue with it to reach the sea wall. Follow the sea wall with the river Stour on your right, soon coming to Judas Gap. At this point most will want to visit Flatford Mill. Turn right across the weir. A well marked path on an elevated wall leads on in a northerly direction to pass Flatford Mill on the opposite bank of the river. This is the lovely view that Constable painted. Continue on to cross the river bridge.

Suitably refreshed retrace your steps across the bridge and turn left downriver. When you come to the weir cross over to the waymarked stile. Turn right over the stile, coming, in a few yards, to a five barred wooden gate and stile and a concrete farm bridge. Cross over the bridge and continue in a southerly direction over a pasture to find after 250 yards a stile, bridge, stile sequence in a hedge. The waymarkers indicate that you have joined circular walk 2 in Dedham.

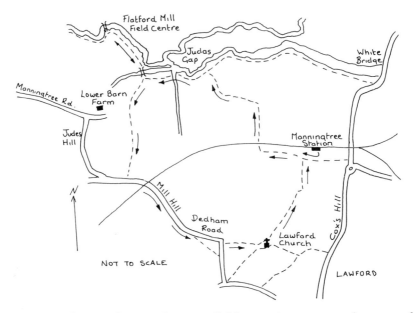

Continue due south over the next field, crossing a stream by way of a bridge with stiles before and after. Now you must climb the hill ahead. There are views of Dedham church on your left if you look back, but the way forward is towards a stile between the fence on your left and the corner of the next field ahead on your right. Having crossed the stile proceed on an elevated green track with the hedge on your right, to a metal gate ahead by a red brick house and on to the road. Turn left and follow the road under a railway bridge.

Now climb up Mill Hill, a one in ten gradient favoured by the local doggy walkers. At the top bear left with the road and just after a right angled bend to the right turn left at a footpath sign. This is Lawford Park in which Lawford Hall and church stand proudly on a hill overlooking Manningtree, the river Stour and Suffolk. Walk the 500 yards to the church and take a look at this building, constructed 600 years ago. It is one of the Essex masterpieces and is thought to be the finest representative in the county of the Decorated style. How was it that a small village church was rebuilt on such a lavish scale early in the 14th century? Lawford Hall too is a fine old building, a timbered house of Armada days. The north east corner of the churchyard permits an exit by foot and a well-defined path leads you delightfully downhill to the track you started on and so back to the station.

Margaretting Tye
The White Hart

The White Hart is about 250 years old and moved to the present site from about 300 yards to the north east. It is known locally as Tigers Island. The 'Island' derived from the fact that when the river Wid flooded and the water rose it never quite reached as high as the pub. The 'Tigers' were the railway builders last century who got dressed up to visit the pub each weekend, and sometimes resolved their disputes in the pub precincts!

I first visited the White Hart in the late sixties and in those days the pub consisted of just the little central building. With the arrival of new owners in the seventies great changes were made. The building was substantially extended, including a large kitchen which to this day enables food to be prepared promptly, a source of great pride, and there is a good choice of items on the menu. A feature is the home-made steak and Guinness pie and also to my taste is the super unsliced crusty bread. At the rear of the building there is a children's room and the single L shaped bar has considerable sitting room. Outdoors at the front, bench tables are in plentiful supply. Nearby, a Victorian post box is reputed to be the oldest in Essex.

The White Hart is a freehouse and real ale buffs will find the Greene King IPA and the Adnams Bitter and Broadside to their liking. Pub hours are 12 noon-2.30 pm, and 6.30 pm-11 pm Monday to Thursday; 12 noon-3 pm and 6 pm-11 pm Friday to Saturday; and 12 noon-2.30 pm and 7 pm-10.30 pm on Sundays. Meals are available till 2 pm in the afternoon and 10 pm in the evening.

Telephone: 01277 840478.

How to get there: Margaretting Tye can be reached from the A12, either from the west through Ingatestone and Margaretting or from the east through Margaretting. In either case turn off the B1002 at the Black Bull public house, signposted to Galleywood. Pass under the railway and immediately after a hump backed bridge, turn right for ¾ mile to reach the hamlet of Margaretting Tye.

Parking: At the pub, but please ask permission to leave your car before setting out on your walk.

Length of the walk: 3¾ miles. OS Map Landranger series 167 Chelmsford and Harlow (GR 684012).

A super walk with some climbs and descents to give the views that usually go with them. Among the points of great interest on the way round are Margaretting church and Hall at the railway level crossing, Canterbury's Farm with free spring water, the Victorian railway tunnel for pedestrians, and the short stroll along part of St. Peters Way.

The Walk

Turn right from the pub along the narrow Swan Lane – watch out for traffic. After ½ mile the road turns sharply left. Our walk route goes straight on by a public bridleway sign. The wide track (sometimes muddy) contours along (south west) with fine views over the Wid valley. Can you spot the square tower of Ingatestone church beyond to the right? At the bottom of Fristling Hall Farm drive continue on to turn right going downhill, following a good track, over the bridge to cross the river Wid and then arriving at Margaretting church.

If you get the chance, do go inside – there is much to admire. The belfry tower, over 400 years old, is a masterpiece of rural craftsmanship, impressive from the outside, overwhelming from the inside. Look for the east window. The fine stained glass is brilliant with colour and human appeal, and has been termed 'the most beautiful glass in Essex'. It represents the Tree of Jesse. A vine stem runs up through three divisions encircling 12 round panels with 24

74

NOT TO SCALE

figures. It was the work of Flemish artists 500 years ago.

To continue the walk, cross the railway line with care at the level crossing. Hereabouts there was a halt used during the Second World War for unloading ammunition which was stored in Rook Wood nearby. After crossing the railway, a footpath sign indicates the right turn just after passing a house. Follow this across a field to Canterbury's Farm, so called because, it is thought, pilgrims to Canterbury passed this way. Observe a 2 ft cubic box-like structure on the left. On opening the box you will see a running spring. it never dries up and is perfectly good to drink. Suitably refreshed, continue north to the road. This is the old A12 at Margaretting, which, having been bypassed, is now the B1002. Turn right and immediately across the road to your left is the Red Lion public house which is well worth a visit. It was a roadhouse in the days of all the traffic but now is rather large for local trade in the village, which has indeed three pubs to cater for a population of 1000!

Passing the Red Lion the road crosses a stream on its way to join the Wid. In a few yards turn right at the footpath sign. From here till almost the end of the walk you are following part of St. Peters Way, a long distance footpath from Chipping Ongar to St. Peters Chapel in Bradwell. Follow the water meadows for 700 yards to the far right hand corner near the railway line. Negotiate the ramp which leads

75

under the railway. This tunnel is probably about 100 years old and accommodates the footpath. A twin tunnel carries the stream. When walking through the tunnel do keep to the centre, as otherwise you may graze your head on the brickwork. This apart, the arrangement makes a safe crossing of the London-Colchester line. Modern roadbuilders could take lessons from our Victorian predecessors!

Emerging from the tunnel, spiral steps lead upwards and then you continue along the side of the stream (south east) to cross a metal bridge over the river Wid. Turn left and follow the river for 500 yards. As it bends to the right, spot a stile and plank bridge and cross this to go uphill for 250 yards. Here turn sharp left and pass in front of a barn and through farm buildings to a farm road. This leads back to the White Hart.

Mill Green
The Cricketers

The Cricketers is a very popular Grays house by the green, where cricket certainly should have been played regularly, even if it wasn't. It is a friendly pub with an enthusiastic welcome for visitors. The floor area was increased by about 50% in 1989 when a tasteful extension was achieved by absorbing a downstairs room into the pub area. In the winter log fires are a welcome feature. Opening times are 12 noon-3 pm and 6 pm-11 pm Mondays to Saturdays, and 12 noon-3 pm and 7 pm-10.30 pm on Sundays. The menu varies frequently but includes a lot of the popular pub fare with frequent specialities including fresh fish daily from Billingsgate, delicious home-made curries and all home-made desserts.

Real ales are Greene IPA and Abbott Ale, both beers served from the barrel, while Red Rock or Thatchers traditional are on offer for the cider lovers. Well behaved dogs are welcome at the Cricketers.

Telephone: 01277 352400.

How to get there: Leave the A12, signposted to Ingatestone, and proceed into the centre of the village. Near the church, go northwards up Fryerning Lane, crossing over the A12 on the way. At the top of the hill turn right past the Woolpack pub. Drive along Mill Green Road for about ½ mile to arrive at the Cricketers on the right.

Parking: The pub car park is at the rear of the building. Please ask before leaving if you want to park your car at the pub while you walk.

Length of the walk: 3½ miles. OS Map Landranger series 167 Chelmsford and Harlow (GR 639012).

Mill Green has been described as 'a heaven on earth' by previous generations. Its name recalls a windmill, the base of which remains. This walk features many open views of a very lovely part of Essex. Come back later to sample the woodland walks to the north of the Cricketers.

The Walk

On leaving the pub turn left along Mill Green Road. Pass Mill Green Cottage and turn left down a lane. On the right are Spinney Cottage, Bracken Cottage, Brookfield Cottage, and finally Slab Cottage – the name mystifies me. At this point there are wide views to the east over Hardings Farm, and the Wid valley to Galleywood church. Turn right over a stile and walk by the lovely gardens of Slab Cottage. A pond has been created in Mill Green Wood on your right. Walk between this and the several ponds on the left to cross a hedge line and on uphill. At the corner of the field turn left with the fence on your right. Join a green track at the next field keeping the hedge on your left, and on reaching Grove Wood keep the wood on your right to walk downhill. The thin radio mast in the woods of Writtle Deer Park to your left was installed for Essex Radio, and then it was found that mid Essex dwellers could just as easily pick up the station on other frequencies.

Turn left at the corner and soon come on your right to a stile and bridge. Having crossed these walk uphill through the wood to Little Hyde Lane where there is a gap in the fence near a gate. Turn right along the lane by Grove Cottage. At a road junction turn left, then in 200 yards turn right into a field by a sign marked 'Courtesy Path leading to Fryerning Lane'. Follow the path across a field, then turn left along the field edge. Towards the bottom of the field walk to the right of a fence into a thicket. Here turn right and follow this path out to Fryerning Lane with, finally, a school on your right (Ingatestone Infants). Turn right up this lane with several large houses on your left.

MILL GREEN

Mapletree Lane

Millgreen Common

The Cricketers P.H

little Hyde la.

Beggar Hill

The Grove

A12

Fryerning Hall

FRYERNING

Fryerning la.

NOT TO SCALE

INGATESTONE

You may choose to walk up the left or right side but join the right side when the path is elevated above the road. When you reach the steps turn left down them and cross the green to walk along the Blackmore Road.

The composition of Fryerning Hall, The Woolpack inn, the church, and the green in this area, with long views to south and east, is likely to stay in your memory. A more detailed examination of the church is justified. The tower is one of the finest examples of 15th century brickwork in the county. The priest's door is also 15th century and the main door is Norman. The churchyard is distinguished by pine and yew trees, and on the north side stands a monument enclosed by iron railings to the memory of members of the Disney family, who died in the 19th century. The famous Walt Disney was descended from those Essex men and women of years ago.

From the main door of the church turn right and at a hedge turn right again walking round the edge of a graveyard to a stile. Cross the stile and continue with a ditch on your right. There are fine views all round as you reach a pond in the corner. A waymarked post directs you across a field going downhill to a lake. Walk through the plantation and turn left along the waterside. At the corner follow the arrow along a path leading to a bridge. Cross the bridge and turn left to the road. Turn right for 350 yards coming to Little Lyndseys and next door a farm track by a concrete footpath sign. Turn right along the track. At the end of a barn turn left through a gate to a field corner. Turn half right (north) crossing diagonally downhill to a stile/bridge/stile combination at the bottom of the field. After negotiating these walk uphill with a fence on your left to another stile. Cross into a wider track between the stream on your left and a market garden on your right. You will soon reach a wide stile and a concrete footpath sign at a road. The Old Beer House is opposite. Even in my time it has been an off licence but now it is a private residence, and the residents of Beggar Hill, for this is the name of the hamlet, have to go further afield for alcoholic refreshment.

Turn right for a few yards and left at a concrete footpath sign. In 5 yards cross a stile, and another after 100 yards. In 30 yards another stile is tucked away on the right by the hedge. After crossing this stile keep to the right of a pond, whilst cutting a corner to reach a gap in the facing hedge. Cross the stile and follow between fences to a field, negotiating two more stiles on the way. Continue uphill (east) bearing to the right of the houses to a stile by a gate next to a concrete footpath sign. Turn right along Mapletree Lane for a few yards. Now turn right at a bridleway sign to walk over the green back to the Cricketers and your car.

Moreton
The White Hart

Moreton is described as a gentle rambling village. This is a perfect description for the walking fraternity although I somehow doubt that it was in that sense intended by the author when he wrote it. In any event the church (which is 13th century) is at one end, whilst the centre of the village is at the other. The White Hart has been welcoming to walkers for over 25 years. Yes, there have been some changes in that time but the friendly hospitality has remained.

Food is served from 11 am-11 pm Monday to Saturday and from 12 noon-10.30 pm on Sunday. The food is home-made and ranges from bar snacks to à la carte in the dining room. Some of the very superior snacks on offer include soft roes on toast and grilled black pudding with cheese.

Real ales are Adnams Bitter, Ridleys IPA, Ridleys Rumpus, Courage Best Bitter and Courage Directors. Bulmers Scrumpy Jack draught cider is on tap.

Telephone: 01277 890228.

How to get there: The B184 runs from Ongar to Leaden Roding. Moreton is signposted off this road to the west either from Fyfield or Shelley just north of Ongar. Both routes are about 2 miles.

Parking: At the pub. There is no objection to leaving your car while you walk but please ask the manager before you set off.

Length of the walk: 3½ miles. OS Map Landranger series 167 Chelmsford and Harlow (GR 538070).

A rewarding walk, first following Cripsey Brook along the water meadows then at a higher elevation back by the field paths to Moreton church, with wide views over the valley.

The Walk

On leaving the pub turn right and right again down the hill and over the quaint little brick bridge across Cripsey Brook. This river flows on to Chipping Ongar where it joins the river Roding. Just past the bridge turn left at a public footpath sign. It is marked Moreton Countryway with a green and yellow arrow. Cross over the stile into tranquil water meadows by the riverside. At one time almost all rivers in Essex were flanked by water meadows like these to absorb the floodwaters but

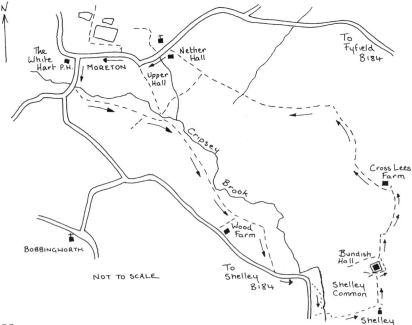

sadly many have been ploughed up.

Continue along the meadows for about ½ mile. There are lovely sights of the sloping banks across the brook. When you reach a stile and bridge ignore the bridge but cross the stile, taking care on the narrow section where the path is close to the edge of the bank. When you reach a field boundary on your right cross a bridge and stile. The correct route at this point is not by the field edge but continues over the middle of the field (south east) to a plank bridge over a ditch. Yes, it's there but you may have to look for it! Go onwards now coming closer to the brook and then reaching a farm track near Wood Farm on your right. Here proceed slightly left of your previous line to a crossing hedge in which there is a bridge and stile. Cross this and continue with a wood on your right. Keep on this line to join the river bank. When the river bends to the left keep straight on. Over the ditch ahead of you there is a plank bridge and a stile. After crossing these look to your right for a large oak tree beside a gate. Walk to this and cross the stile behind the tree.

Turn left and walk along the road for a few yards. You pass the interesting Gothic Cottage, and after passing another large oak tree cross the stile in the hedge on your left. Here the right of way follows an old hedge line where the hedge has been removed. Walk half right to a post which has a yellow waymark arrow on it. From the post turn right and walk south for 200 yards directly to a metal bridge. Cross the brook and continue straight on to the main hedge opposite. Turn right to a large gate with a blue arrow on it. After negotiating the gate soon turn left along a grassy track. At the end of the field on the left, turn left along the hedge to Bundish Hall and walk round the south and east walls of the property. The bridleway continues on its well-defined way with right and left bends till arriving at Cross Lees Farm. Turn left in front of a black shed (when we were there last it was full of noisy turkeys). Walk along the side of the shed till you reach a narrow farm track. Turn right and follow this past paddocks on your right where there are usually some magnificent tall ponies. Bear left towards a large oak tree and pass through the gap in the hedge beside it. Follow along a wide grass margin with the paddocks continuing on your right. When the paddocks stop a fine hedge takes over guardianship of the next field. There are sloes, and red berries in abundance (if you are there in autumn). Make for the corner of this field and pass over a narrow earth bridge.

Now be careful! Turn right almost 90°. Spot a tree on the left edge of the remains of a hedge, just west of due north from where you are. Walk to this tree. Now turn half left and walk north west about the same distance again. Your aim is to reach the T junction of two well-defined tracks but if you come to a crossing track only it will be necessary to reconnoitre to find the T. Continue on the track which follows the westerly route. Now it's easy! Follow this track enjoying the wide views of Nether Hall and Moreton church ahead and Bobbingworth to your left. After ⅔ mile walk past the farm out to the road.

Turn left, soon reaching the church, which you may wish to inspect. Next to it is the magnificent rectory with a huge garden for the vicar's attention. Continue along the village street passing the police house and the primary school to the centre. You come first to the Moreton Massey which has been used in a Lovejoy television episode. In this show our pub, the White Hart, was on camera and looked quite superb. So ends our visit to Moreton, a little known village in Essex, but I am sure you will agree well worth a return trip.

Mountnessing
The Prince of Wales

The Prince of Wales stands on a Roman road which was built in the 3rd century. The building that stood on the site at the time was mentioned in the Domesday Book. For several hundred years it was a bakery, drawing its flour supplies from the windmill nearby, and the original baker's ovens are still at the rear of the pub. During the 19th century the road outside was turnpiked, and a list of charges was displayed on a plaque outside the toll house. Part of the plaque is now displayed in the Prince of Wales. The exterior of the house with its bay windows and shutters has a slight French appearance, and it has been a landmark to countless motorists in Essex.

Excellent food is available, both meals and bar snacks, and children are catered for. Favourites on the menu are beef and venison pie, locally cured ham on the bone and spicy chicken wings.

The Prince of Wales is a Ridleys house and Ridleys IPA, Ridleys Rumpus and Ridleys ESX are usually available, together with Strongbow cider. The pub is open for all food and drink during

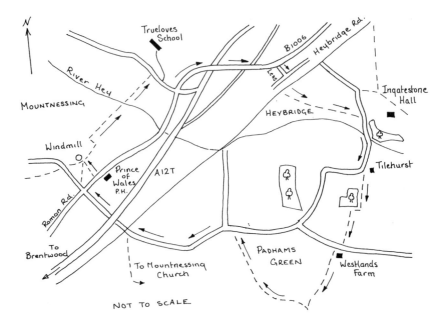

the hours 11 am-3 pm and 6 pm-11 pm Monday-Saturday, 12 noon-3 pm and 7 pm-10.30 pm on Sundays. During the week you may find the pub closed for part of the afternoon.

Telephone: 01277 353445.

How to get there: Mountnessing lies just off the A12, 3½ miles to the north east of Brentwood or 1½ miles to the south west of Ingatestone. The magnificent windmill is a landmark. The Prince of Wales faces the playing fields which surround the mill.

Parking: At the pub, though this is limited. There are other nearby areas in Thoby Lane and also by the village hall near the mill.

Length of the walk: 4½ miles. OS Map Landranger series 167 Chelmsford and Harlow (GR 632979).

A walk of great variety which passes the historic windmill, and the beautiful Ingatestone Hall. We twice make the crossing of the very busy A12 with the help of overflying minor roads. In between there is the joy of the scarcely touched 'back country' through Padhams Green between Ingatestone and Mountnessing.

The Walk

Leave the pub, cross the road, and head for the windmill. This was lovingly restored in the 70s and 80s by Essex County Council and many local volunteers. It is probably the finest surviving post mill in the county and is on display on certain days during the year. To the right of the mill walk towards a gap in the hedge (north east). Through the hedge continue in the same direction. Often this path is defined by the farmer. It leads for about 800 yards to a concrete footbridge. If it is not defined, aim to the right of Trueloves School which faces you at a distance of ¾ mile. Cross the bridge (over the river Hey) and walk uphill to a footpath signpost on Trueloves Lane.

Turn right and walk down to a T junction. Turn left to cross over the A12. About a 100 yards further on turn right down the road called the Leas and at the end turn right along Heybridge Road. Very soon a footpath sign on the left indicates a path between houses, leading to a level crossing. After carefully negotiating this, a good path between fields for ½ mile leads to a footpath sign at Hall Lane.

Diverting to the left for a few yards we come to the magnificent Ingatestone Hall. This is the ancestral home of the Petres. The site had been a nunnery of Barking and came into the hands of Sir William Petre in 1539. The hall was completed by 1548 and, despite many subsequent additions and demolitions, it is still one of the loveliest Essex houses, with its characteristic Elizabethan stepped gables. Having been closed to the public for many years, it is now open again (Easter Saturday to the last Sunday in September from 1 pm to 6 pm. It is open on Bank Holiday Mondays but otherwise closed on Mondays and Tuesdays). You may therefore be able to combine a visit with your walk.

To continue the walk, retrace your steps and walk along Hall Lane (south) passing Tilehurst, another interesting house built in the 19th century. At the T junction cross over slightly to your left to follow a bridleway sign, passing Kitchen Wood to reach Westlands Farm. Turn right up the road and then left at the bridleway sign. After 500 yards on reaching a thicket take the path to the right and follow this to the hamlet of Padhams Green. At a T junction turn left and follow this lane. Take the opportunity to admire the views over the Wid valley to your left and over Heybridge towards Fryerning to your right. Follow the road signs to Mountnessing, avoiding several left and right turns to cross over the railway and the A12 back to the village.

Mountnessing church, as is often the case, is at some distance from the village though it can easily be reached on foot in ½ hour. From the pub walk back over the railway turning right off the road at a footpath sign to follow a path which is usually defined through the crops. The church makes a good picture alongside the Georgian

Mountnessing Hall, a seven bay brick building. It has been refashioned from the one the Normans built, and the Roman tiles and masonry they used are visible in the walls. The church is at the crossroads of no less than five footpaths going off in all directions. This demonstrates how often in olden times paths were used by worshippers. Nowadays on a Sunday morning one comes upon churches surrounded by motor cars – when we approach the same churches as walkers on other days of the week, the thought is there that we see these lovely buildings in a more traditional setting.

Navestock Side
The Green Man

The Green Man is an impressive looking building standing opposite a cricket green. It was here that the Essex Cricket Club was formed in 1790 and from these beginnings one of the leading county cricket teams of England has grown. The Green Man, which first became a pub in 1620, was previously a hunting lodge for the Dudbrook estate – the 'big' house is less than a mile away. A bistro-style restaurant occupies the stable block, and the carriage building, subsequently a cricket pavilion, is now a function room. The main building features three separate bars with high ceilings, comfortably furnished and carpeted throughout. Walkers are welcome inside this unique pub, and families with young children can be served in the bistro.

If it's beer you are after there is Adnams and Tetley Bitter, both on handpump. With the availability of all the usual bar snacks and the bistro, most appetites will be catered for. Specialities include grilled swordfish, and sirloin Navestock – the latter a steak stuffed with mushrooms, onions and garlic. The pub is open during the hours 11 am-3 pm and 6 pm-11 pm Monday to Saturday, 12 noon-10.30 pm on Sundays. The kitchen is closed all day Monday and also Sunday evenings. Telephone: 01277 372231.

How to get there: Navestock Side is about 3 ½ miles to the north west of Brentwood. Take the A128 from Brentwood towards Ongar. Before you get there Navestock Side is signposted to the left.

Parking: At the pub or nearby on the south end of the green.

Length of the walk: 4 miles. OS Map Landranger series 167 Chelmsford and Harlow (GR 564975).

An excellent walk on a hilly part of Essex. There are long views to the north over the Roding valley and beyond to Stanford Rivers and Toot Hill. During the walk you will pass Dudbrook, an elegant country house. Over Beacon Hill deer are often seen. Just off the route is the beautifully sited Navestock church, the spire an imaginative recreation after wartime devastation. Towards the end of the walk at the east end of Lower Boishall Wood a submerged well is said to date from Roman times.

The Walk

Leaving the pub, turn left. Two public footpath signs stand together at the corner of the bistro. Take the one pointing diagonally across the fields towards a large white house (Dudbrook). Walk across the field aiming for the house in the distance on a path now reinstated by the farmer. After about 400 yards the path goes downhill to reach a steep sided stream. Here you will find a little bridge with a metal handrail. The bridge is about 700 yards from the start of the walk. After crossing the bridge go uphill, slightly to the right, across a field, reaching a thicket to the right of Dudbrook. The path goes through a gap in the thicket to a road. Cross the road and continue uphill along a lane signposted 'Howard Lodge'. Cross another lane soon reaching Beacon Hill Farm. Turn left off the road, and walk downhill through farm buildings. Continue down the field side.

On this descent from Beacon Hill groups of deer are often met. They inhabit many of the small woods which are a feature of Navestock parish. At the bottom of the field, you find a peaceful spot, with birdsong and far from the traffic. Here the path goes left and then right up a good track to reach the road at a footpath sign. Pause here to take in the glorious sights which abound, especially if you have chosen a sunny day. Through the trees to the left is Bois Hall, while over your right shoulder to the north the river Roding and the shining

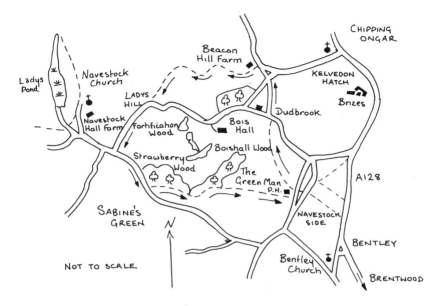

spire of Stanford Rivers church can be spotted.

Our route is forward along the direction you have been walking, but now on a lane (Ladys Hill) and descending quite rapidly. At the bottom the route turns left at a T junction. If you wish to visit Navestock church turn right for 500 yards. The depressed area (now a rose garden) in front of the church is the result of an enemy landmine falling on 21st September 1940. It was caught in a tree so exploded above ground causing extensive damage. One wonders at the strength of the medieval structure which stood up to the blast.

To continue the walk, retrace your steps to the T junction at the bottom of Ladys Hill. Proceed for 450 yards going south eastwards to leave the road at a footpath sign on the left. Walk over rough ground for a few yards with hedge and road on your right, and the delightfully named Strawberry Wood on your left. On reaching a field continue beside the wood on the field edge to reach and cross a bridge. Near the corner of the field cross into the field on the left. Soon there is a big gap between the end of the wood on your right (Gipsy Bottom) and the next wood (Lower Boishall). Turn right up this greenway and follow to the end of the woods. Go out into the field and take the path on the left walking for a further 3/5 mile back to the Green Man. You pass a narrow strip of woodland on your left. Just beyond this, if the field is not in crop, you may spot some indications of the submerged Roman well.

Pattiswick
The Compasses

Pattiswick has always struck me as a pretty name but the experts tell us that the word simply means Paetti's dwelling place. It was clearly a parish with the usual ingredients – a church, a school, a pub, a few farms, and a few farm cottages, spread over several acres to the south of the woodland area around Marks Hall, to the east of Stisted and to the west of Coggeshall. I say 'was' because it is now amalgamated with Bradwell parish, which the walk also visits, and, though the buildings have been preserved, we have a privatised school, a privatised church, and a privatised rectory! Some of the old farms near the route are Harveys, 16th century, Whiteshill, 15th century, and the church, 14th century.

Perhaps not quite so venerable is the Compasses, though there are 400 year old beams in the Hunters bar. It is a freehouse and family owned, and is indeed a fine country pub both for eating and drinking in, drawing guests from far around. The establishment is children friendly so that meals can be eaten with the family in all rooms. There is a substantial garden which can be enjoyed when the weather is right and a hedged section that can be very pleasant to sit in even on windy days.

Opening times are 11 am-2.30 pm and 6 pm-11 pm on Mondays to Saturdays, 12 noon-3 pm and 7 pm-10.30 pm on Sundays. Meals are served from 12 noon-2.30 pm and 7 pm-10 pm throughout the week. Among the many tempting dishes available are tuna fish and pasta bake, spicy barbecue ribs of pork, and giant filled Yorkshire puddings. There is a comprehensive selection of food, including vegetarian meals and bar snacks. The menu is displayed on blackboards and items, many of which are unusual and innovative, are changed frequently. Real ales are Greene King IPA and Abbott, and Rayments, while Taunton Blackthorn cider is on draught.

Telephone: 01376 561322.

How to get there: Approach by way of the A120. If coming from the east pass round the north of Coggeshall. A mile further on take a minor road signposted Pattiswick to the right (north) of the A120. If coming from Braintree, just past Bradwell village the same road to Pattiswick is signed to the left (north). Barely a mile up this road you pass the church on your right and the Compasses is less than ½ mile further on.

Parking: There is good parking at the Compasses, and the landlord has no problem with you leaving your car for a couple of hours. However please let him know you are doing so before embarking on your walk.

Length of the walk: 4½ miles. OS Map Landranger series 168 Colchester and the Blackwater (GR 820247).

A splendid walk – downhill from Pattiswick Hall to the river Blackwater with views all around. A short river walk gets you to Bradwell Hall and church. Then by the river and Whites Hill to Doghouse Road and the village.

The Walk

Turn left down Compasses Road, soon turning right at a bridleway sign along a wide green lane flanked by two hedges. In 350 yards you come to a small wood named Acre Piece and turn left down a farm lane. As you approach Harvey's Farm the lane becomes metalled and you follow it turning right and left. Now pass Pattiswick Hall Farm and Hall with Pattiswick church over the field to your left. On reaching Doghouse Road where there is a phone box, a post box, and a black footpath sign No. 45, turn right down the footpath and walk south west across the field on a well-defined track going downhill. There are wide views over the Blackwater valley as you walk (crossing two hedges on the way) for nearly ¾ mile to the Coggeshall road. This is Stane Street, a Roman road. Turn left along the road and walk for barely 400 yards to the end of a row of houses. Cross the road to a footpath sign at the side of the garage and continue downhill for a few yards to turn left into the next field down a steep little slope. Now turn right and follow the field edge round to the left with a hedge on your right.

After about ½ mile the path turns right and 500 yards later you turn right off the path and cross a broad farm bridge over the river Blackwater to climb past Bradwell Hall to the church. This is the typical Norman church in a remote parish. If access is available, there are notable wall paintings dating from 1320. The setting of the Hall and church by the river is delightful. Turn left along Church Road for 250 yards and at a concrete footpath sign turn left through woodland to cross a concrete bridge over the river Blackwater. Very soon turn

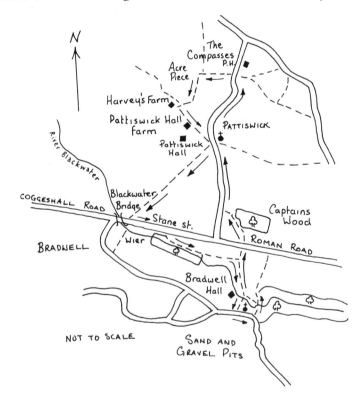

left along a field edge passing the bridge which led to the church.

Retrace your steps until the path turns sharply to the left. Here turn right to walk uphill (north) to the Coggeshall road (Whites Hill farm is on your right across the field). Cross the road with care to a stile, a gate and a concrete footpath sign. Continue uphill to the corner of a wood on Whites Hill. Now walk uphill with the wood on your right. At the end of the field turn left with the field edge on your left along a wide green track, reaching Doghouse Road in a very few yards. Turn right, still climbing, and follow this road, passing Agers Cottage on the right.

Take the road signposted to Stisted and Halstead, passing Wren Cottage set nicely back, to reach Pattiswick church. Though parts of the building are 700 years old, this church has been sold as a private residence. However, despite the building being fenced off, the churchyard is of course holy ground and can still be passed through by walkers. Continue along the road passing the Old Schoolhouse, also in private hands. Further up the road is the Old Rectory neatly placed halfway between the church and the Compasses! To the right is Church Farm, and the last 400 yards takes you back to your car.

Pleshey
The White Horse

Pleshey comes from an old French word, plesseis, meaning an enclosed space. This name was given by the Normans – in Saxon times the area was known as 'Tumblestown'. To this day all the dwellings in the village are within the castle's ramparts, which measure one mile in circumference. Yes, the Normans built the castle, but they built it on the earthworks of a mount and moated court that the Saxons laid out and the Saxons used the enclosure formed by the rampart and ditch thrown up by the Ancient Britons. Altogether the earthworks at Pleshey are some of the most remarkable in the land. Six hundred years ago Pleshey enjoyed its richest period with its own mayor, market and over 40 shops. Its lord was the Duke of Gloucester, Lord High Constable of England, and uncle to King Richard II and the castle was a place of power, wealth, and pageantry. Gardens, deer parks, and parkland stretched for many miles. In 1397 Richard, resentful of his uncle's power, visited Pleshey and had him lured away to be seized and later murdered in Calais. I am confident that your visit to Pleshey will be more peaceful!

The White Horse dates back to the late 15th century and still maintains much of its former character. Some of the original timbers and flooring can still be seen in the present bar and outhouse, these two buildings being joined together by a slate roof. The original roof timbers can also be seen upstairs. Later additions were made to the building to provide the kitchen area and the toilets. Opening hours are 11 am-3 pm and 7 pm-11 pm on Mondays to Fridays, 11 am-11 pm Saturdays and 12 noon-10.30 pm on Sundays. Food is served throughout opening times. A full à la carte menu is provided in the restaurant and offers a variety of dishes, including steaks, duck, fish, venison, and fowl. The bar menu has something for everyone, with choices ranging from White Horse pie to lasagne, chilli or jacket potatoes. There is a children's menu – and a vegetarian menu.

The real ale which is regularly available in this freehouse is Nethergate Umble Ale from Clare. Others frequently on tap are Ridleys and Tolly Cobbold. Guest beers are also usually available.

Telephone: 01245 237281.

How to get there: Pleshey can be reached from the A130 either at Ford End or through Howe Street. The White Horse is at the top of the village near the church.

Parking: Plenty of room at the pub, but do ask before leaving your car to set out on the walk.

Length of the walk: 4¼ miles. OS Map Landranger series 167 Chelmsford and Harlow (GR 663143).

No single walk can do full justice to Pleshey which possesses a network of pathways to be proud of. All the more reason to make a return visit to the White Horse, and try another walk off the map.

The Walk

On leaving the White Horse turn left and walk down 'The Street'. You pass the little lane leading to the castle, the site of which is now, alas, accessible only by arrangement with the agents. The buildings in the village are all of interest. Turn left after 200 yards. Take heed of a small water pump on the corner with a recently added railing 'to commemorate the Queen's Silver Jubilee in 1977'. Further down this road, which will be later marked Back Lane, there is something quite unusual – Pleshey Forge. If you are lucky, the smithy may be shoeing

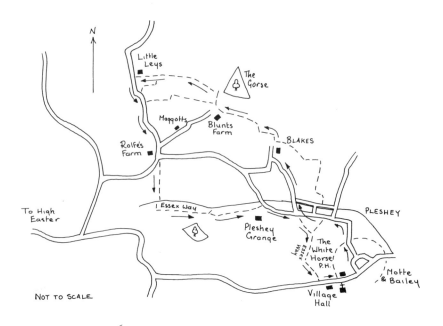

a horse when you go by. Past the forge turn left and there is a children's playing field tucked away on your right.

Follow the lane downhill beyond the ditch enclosing the village. Keep on this road, turning left as you go. When you see a concrete public bridleway post pointing up a wide grass lane to the left, turn right along a narrow lane, first passing Blakes Cottage then a few hundred yards later arrive at Blakes Farm, a big house recently sheltered by a high brick wall. Pass Blakes on your right and follow a good green lane. When you join a crossing track turn left. This lane is used by tractors and leads you towards Blunts Farm. The hedge on the left disappears for the last field.

At the farm continue over the concrete yard, saying hello to the chickens. The concrete track continues, bearing right past a pond, to the Gorse which is the name for the wood on your right. Here turn left along a concrete path with a hedge on your left. When the track turns right keep on over rough ground to join a headland path with wide views all round including Pleshey church over to your left. The area between field and hedge widens. As you approach the farm ahead (Little Leys) you cross a gap in the facing hedge, where, if there is still no bridge, you will have to negotiate the ditch. After one more little field you walk between the hedge and the farm buildings and leave the farm for the road.

Turn left and after 175 yards left again, signposted to Pleshey. Ignore the lane signposted to Maggotts and walk on past Rolfe's farmhouse. At the crossroads briefly follow the road signposted to High Easter before turning left (south) down a well-defined track at a byway sign. After 650 yards you will meet a crossing track. Turn left along this (another byway). It is the Essex Way, a good and well-walked track. It later becomes hedged and Parsonage Brook is one field to the left. You pass by a farm (Woods) to join a lane. Continue on this lane past Pleshey Grange (a large house with a fine tree lined drive). Now the church stands proudly on your right.

Three hundred yards from the Grange turn up a wide green lane (a public bridleway). When you reach a road turn left past Pleshey village hall and soon after the church. This building dates back to the 19th century, rebuilt by the Tuffnells of Langleys in Great Waltham. The previous one was from the 14th century and its demise was another chapter in the Pleshey story. The ill fated Duke of Gloucester founded a college of nine chaplains in the church. With the passing of the monasteries, Sir John Gates, to whom it had passed, chose to destroy all the medieval buildings. The most significant relic of those times is a stone in the wall of the present church with the name of Richard II inscribed on it in Latin. This probably came from the castle. The White Horse lies just beyond the church on the left.

Purleigh
The Bell

Purleigh is a most attractive village, idyllic and sleepy. Originally it was all contained on the top of Church Hill, but now has spread to the low hill below. However the church shares the hill top with the pub and a few houses. Some years ago a few hundred yards south of the pub it was thought that remains had been found of the castle but this has yet to be validated. The Bell, with wonderful views from the garden of the Dengie peninsula, comprises the combination of several houses, one of which was the priests house, probably occupied by Lawrence Washington, the great-great-grandfather of George, the father of the USA. The pub is now a 16th century grade II listed building in a conservation area. Barry and Julie Mott were both born and brought up in the village and after some time living away returned home to purchase the Bell, which is a walker friendly and welcoming pub.

Opening hours are 12 noon-3 pm and 7 pm-10.30 pm on Sundays, 12 noon-3 pm and 6 pm-11 pm for the rest of the week. Food is available 12 noon-1.45 pm and 7.30 pm-9.30 pm on Mondays and from

Wednesdays to Saturdays. On Sundays it is on offer from 12 noon-1.45 pm and 7.30 pm-9 pm. The kitchen is closed on Tuesdays. In addition to the usual main meals and bar snacks, various home-made savoury pies are a feature. Turning to the drinks, four real ales are on draught: Adnams Bitter, Greene King IPA, Friary Meux and a guest beer. Copperhead draught cider is also available. Children are allowed in the garden only. Dogs however are welcome in the bar providing they behave themselves!

Telephone: 01621 828348.

How to get there: Purleigh is signposted off the large roundabout on the A414 south east of Danbury. Follow the B1010 into the village centre and take the left turn up to the church, beside which is the Bell.

Parking: At the pub but please ask permission from the landlord before setting out on your walk.

Length of the walk: 3 ¾ miles. OS Map Landranger series 168 Colchester and the Blackwater (GR 842020).

A lovely little walk. Purleigh and environs have hilly bits, modestly above sea level but enabling spectacular views over the Blackwater estuary and the Dengie peninsula.

The Walk
After leaving the Bell, walk through the churchyard. You may be able to visit the church before or after your walk. All Saints is famous for having had as rector Lawrence Washington. Lawrence was appointed in 1632 but replaced in 1643. American money in memory of the Washingtons enabled the church to be restored in 1892. Leave the churchyard and turn left (west) for a few yards. Turn right at a footpath sign, scrambling through a thicket to a stile. Cross the stile and walk along the edge of a field with the hedge on your left. After 175 yards a defined path goes downhill to a gate. Cross the road to the New Hall vineyard and continue through the farm buildings. New Hall is one of the leading English winemakers and their German style wines are well worth sampling.

The path proceeds along the field edge through a wide gap into the next field and over a stile. At this point aim half left (north west) to the left projection of the oncoming field hedge (the path is usually reinstated by the farmer). Cross a stile and then negotiate a rather poor fence crossing to enter a hedged path. You will emerge from this onto a muddy tractor track. Turn right along this for a few yards and left round the hedge end. Find and cross a plank bridge into the field on the left. Here turn right and follow the path with a ditch on your right

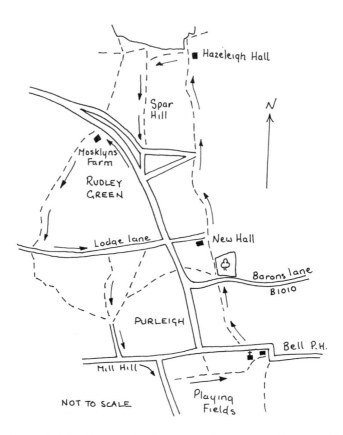

Hazeleigh Hall

Spar
Hill

N

Mosklyns
Farm

Rudley
Green

Lodge lane

New Hall

Barons lane
B1010

Purleigh

Bell P.H.

Mill Hill

NOT TO SCALE

Playing
Fields

through two fields. On coming to a farm steading continue over a stile in a wooden fence to Hazeleigh Hall. Almost opposite the front door of this attractive building turn left and follow the drive out past a pond on the left for 175 yards beyond, to two concrete signs standing together. Take the bridleway on the left (south) which soon joins a hedge on its right. This route ascends Spar Hill, a modest height indeed, but with clear views towards Osea Island, Bradwell towers in the background, and a few miles further on just to the right of Bradwell, the tiny square outline of St. Peter's Chapel, built in AD 654.

Descend from Spar Hill to reach the road. Turn right for 350 yards to Mosklyns Farm. Enter the farm at a home-made footpath sign to the right of a gate. Cross a concrete slab and follow a path, with a fence on the left and a pond on the right, to a wooden gate. Through the gate go straight on through the field to the corner. Cross through a rather primitive stile marked No. 17 (footpath). Continue uphill straight on to a black and white pole with a large 'F' on top. The pole is to the left of a pond. Cross the stile by the black and white pole and walk from here to another large 'F' close to a metal gate at the end of the field. Cross a stile into the road at a metal footpath sign.

Turn left along this minor road (Lodge Lane) for 550 yards to a concrete byway sign on the right. Follow the byway downhill for 80 yards then there is a sharp little climb for 350 yards through the green lane to the top. Carry on down to a road (Mill Hill). Turn left and walk down to Purleigh village.

Turn right along the road signposted Cold Norton. Go left (east) into the playing field and exit by the far left hand corner into a field. Now the last climb of the day to a stile, approached by very impressive steps. This leads into the churchyard where you began.

Stanford Rivers
The White Bear

The White Bear has a lovely garden which leads down to the river Roding – lively at the weekend but an idyllic spot during the week when it is at its most peaceful. Formerly a tied house belonging to Allied Breweries it is now a freehouse joining a small group of pubs in the district. Bar hours are 11 am-3 pm and 6 pm-11 pm Mondays to Fridays, 11 am-11 pm Saturdays and 12 noon-10.30 pm Sundays. Traditional and tasty pub fare is the order of the day – snacks, ploughman's, pies, steaks, scampi and so on. The White Bear, which used to stand by the roadside has benefited from the 'bypass', which effectively moved the road 50 yards away. It has plenty of parking space. The real ales available are Greene King IPA and Abbott Ale, and Taunton Blackthorn Cider is on tap.

Telephone: 01277 362185.

How to get there: The White Bear is in a group of two pubs and an engineering works on the A113 between Ongar and Passingford

Bridge, approximately 2¾ miles from either. It is situated about 50 yards off the south side of the road and the turn off is signposted at the roadside.

Parking: At the pub. Please ask permission before you set out on the walk.

Length of the walk: 4 miles. OS Map Landranger series 167 Chelmsford and Harlow (GR 532998).

This is a walk to remember. Starting at the river Roding, we gently climb through what had been classic parkland to Navestock church and on up to Navestock Heath, before marching them down again to Shonks Mill! Do think of taking binoculars to see all the views to perfection.

The Walk

Coming out of the pub turn to your right. A footpath sign indicates a path which crosses a low stile and follows the side of the pub property to the south east. At the rear of the pub walk south for about 150 yards to the river Roding and cross a bridge. In this area behind the pub there is a car boot sale on Saturday mornings and a clay pigeon shooting club on Sunday mornings. Both can be passed through in the early part of the day, the shooters being careful to stop while you pass. The noise may disturb your enjoyment of part of the walk but both events are finished by 2 pm.

The Roding is a typical Essex river, much cleaner than it was 20 years ago, but no longer populated by otters as it once was. After crossing the bridge, which has a humped concrete base of some antiquity, look to the south east over this large field. You may be able to detect a gap in the woods. Head for this on a 600 yard trek – it will become more apparent as you cross the field. On reaching the woods the track becomes well defined. Follow this path past the wood on your right. When it parts from the wood keep to the side of the trees and follow along close to a large lake – Ladys Pond. This was an ornamental water created in Georgian times as part of the classic landscape leading from Navestock Hall to the river. Sadly the Hall, which was once close by the church, is no longer there. It is sometimes suggested that walkers should keep to the wide track, but be assured the definitive path is much nearer the fisherman's path. Continue on your line and when the lake bends to the right, walk half left to join the main track. Pass the farm buildings and come to the church. It is this church which is described in the walk from Navestock Side, and it is well worth a visit.

To continue the walk carry on along the road. Turn right and follow

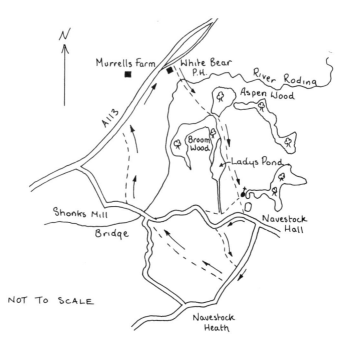

Murrells Farm White Bear
                P.H.
                        River Roding
                Aspen Wood

A113

Broom
Wood
                Ladys Pond

Shonks Mill
                                Navestock
Bridge   Hall

NOT TO SCALE

                Navestock
                Heath

this road for 400 yards round a left hand bend. Take the crossfield
path on the left at a footpath signpost near a telephone pole. Aim to
the left of a line of trees facing you 350 yards up the hill. Go through
the gap into the next field and follow the field edge with the hedge
on your right to the road. Turn right and walk up the road for 400
yards. Opposite the last pair in a row of houses you will see a footpath
sign pointing back downhill (north west). Before taking this path you
may wish to look at the large common at Navestock Heath ahead of
you a few yards. Round to your left on the heath is the Plough public
house which, if open, will provide sustenance. Suitably refreshed,
retrace your steps to restart from the previously noted signpost.

Begin with the hedge on your right. The path does not follow the
hedge line but crosses the field diagonally to go past Yew Tree Farm
ahead on your left. Now pass the left hand edge of an incomplete
hedge facing you, and continue ever downwards with super views of
the Roding valley to reach a footpath sign at the corner of Shonk's Mill
Road and Mill Lane. Pause here to inspect the sight of the old mill, the
new road bridge, and the dry river bed with the 500 yard long
diversion carrying the water. Cross the new bridge and the river

bridge and soon climb down off the road at a footpath sign in a hedge. Follow the river course when it bends to the right, but when it bends again continue in a northerly direction to a house ahead just left of Stoneyrocks Plantation. Turn left down the drive to the busy road ahead. Turn right along a wide verge and walk the ½ mile passing Traceys Farm and Murrells Farm on your left, and finally the Woodman public house on your right before arriving back at the White Bear.

Stebbing
The White Hart

Stebbing is a village as old as the Domesday book, and probably much older. It has a moated mound more aged than William the Conqueror, and an abundance of cottages and farms, over 50 of which have been there for 300 years, many much more than that. The house by the mound is 16th century. There is a 15th century cottage by the churchyard gate. The church is early 14th century and a testament to the builders and craftsmen who created it, just before the advent of the Black Death.

Not quite so ancient but still over 500 years is the White Hart itself. It is a beautiful old building with the public area on two levels. The lower level now serves mainly as a restaurant, whilst the upper level has a long bar with several wooden backed stools. The pub includes what was the downstairs room of a tiny cottage at the north end of the building. In fact this is now the pool room! Between there and the main bar is the famous double sided fireplace, with one fire using one chimney serving two rooms. Did any cottage resident of years ago ever crawl through the fire place to slake his thirst?

Opening times are 11 am-3 pm and 6 pm-11 pm on Mondays to Fridays, 11 am-11 pm on Saturdays, and 12 noon-10.30 pm on Sundays. Good traditional pub food is available every day (but not on Sunday evenings), cutting off at 2 pm and 9.30 pm. Steaks, chops and mixed grills are deliciously prepared on a charcoal grill and a roast lunch is served on Sundays – almost all the food is home-made.

Real ales on draught are Greene King IPA and a guest beer. Taunton Blackthorn cider is on tap. Children are welcome with their parents in the restaurant. Dogs are allowed in the bar if well behaved and there is a small garden area at the back. There are, of course, persistent local rumours of a ghost at the inn!

Telephone: 01371 856383.

How to get there: Approach from Stane Street, the Roman road (A120) between Great Dunmow and Rayne. From either direction Stebbing is signposted north off the main road. Having taken this route you will arrive at Stebbing church. Turn into the village street and soon you will come to the White Hart.

Parking: There is parking behind the pub. You may leave your car there whilst doing the walk but please ask before doing so. There is also the opportunity to park on the street.

Length of the walk: 3 miles. OS Map Landranger series 167 Chelmsford and Harlow (GR 661243).

A short walk passing many of the components of this ancient village, man made and otherwise. There is something about the setting of Stebbing which makes the new visitor feel comfortable on arrival. I am sure that having discovered this delightful village you will want to return again and again.

The Walk

Emerging from the White Hart turn right and right again, walking downhill past a bowling green on your left. Just past the United Reform church on the left, turn right at a concrete footpath sign and enter a cricket field by a green gate. Keep round the left hand side of the pitch and follow to a kissing gate at a gap in the hedge, diagonally opposite the field entrance. There is a wire fence on your left, which you follow crossing a concrete bridge. A large pond is to your left and above it 'The Mount', a moated mound, which is the site of a castle from Norman times, one of those which predated the Conqueror. Above you on your right stands the old village school with the bell still hanging in place.

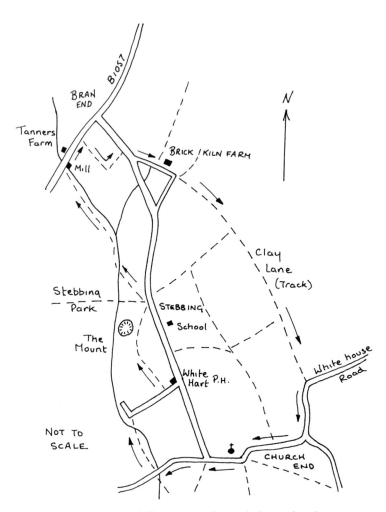

The path continues uphill over a stile and through a kissing gate to the gates of Stebbing Park. The house at the bottom of the drive dates from Shakespearean times. Cross the drive and go over a stile. Walk downhill half left (north west) in the downs across a field which often contains sheep and a few young Highland cattle. Cross the hedge by a metal gate and go over a bridge made from a metal tube. The meadows you are now crossing are between a stream on the left and the Stebbing Brook on the right, and are often full of birdlife. Go past the left side of the mill building, negotiating a red metal gate, and reach the road. Tanners Farm is opposite with a very large pond. Turn right

110

past the mill and cross a bridge over the brook.

Just past a house named Copstones turn right along a track on the left side of the house. At the end of the garden continue with the track across a field. At the end of the field turn left along the field edge out to a road. Turn right past Appledore, an attractive old house. A hundred yards further on turn left off the road signposted to Brick Kiln Lane and Clay Lane. Continue past Brick Kiln Farm to Clay Lane, a wide green lane with ditches on both sides. Follow this fine lane for nearly ¾ mile (south east). Stebbing church is always in prospect over the fields to your right. You reach a lane (Whitehouse Road) at a house called Langcroft. Walk along the lane passing Stebbing Tennis Club. At the T junction turn right past Olde Tree Cottage and soon reach the church.

If you have the opportunity, take time to view the church, with its handsome doorways. The jewel in the crown is the stone rood screen under the chancel arch, but there are many other items to be admired. Leave the church and rejoin the road. There used to be three pubs in Stebbing and the third is beside the church – now a private house named Red Lion House. Continue your walk downhill past the magnificent Tudor building opposite with its beautiful pond beyond the farm buildings. At the bottom of the hill look back at the church to admire how well it is placed to look over the valley. Cross the Stebbing Brook, and at a concrete footpath sign on the right, go over a stile and down two steps. The path leads on to a plank bridge over a ditch, and round to the right you recross the brook by way of a long concrete bridge. Turn left for a further few yards to cross another concrete bridge. Here there is a fine view above of the timbered building of Tan Farm. Walk up the hill, passing several interesting buildings, to arrive back at the White Horse.

Stock
The Hoop

Stock is a pretty village at the southern border of the borough of Chelmsford. The inhabitants are an integration of country folk, many of whose families have lived there for generations, with newcomers, often commuters to the city. The village has a great many public footpaths leaving in all directions, and, as well as the walk described in this book, readers may wish to follow other routes armed with an Ordnance Survey map.

The Hoop is a wonderful little pub, with a big welcome for walkers. Its internal and external appearance has changed little over the last 12 years, though a wall alteration has brought a small room into the public domain. In days gone by the Hoop was a beer house, not being licensed to serve wines and spirits. Now of course it possesses a full licence and on Mondays to Saturdays it is open 11 am to 11 pm. Sundays 12 noon to 10.30 pm. Nevertheless, a high proportion of the customers are 'beer buffs', only here for the beer, and rightly so for there is a good selection of ale, often including names which are unobtainable elsewhere in the county. Nowadays there are usually about six draught beers available in this freehouse: Adnams Bitter and Broadside, and frequently changing guest beers. Scrumpy and Dry Blackthorn cider are also served. Go there around the Spring bank holiday when the annual Beer Festival is held and your choice of beers will have grown to 120 or more! Excellent home cooked food is offered throughout opening hours and it is therefore possible to have a meal in the Hoop at any time between 11 am and 11 pm Monday to Saturday. Dishes include a tempting selection of home-made soups, fish pie and meat dishes. Behind the building is a large garden with service from the back of the pub, so this can be perfect when the weather is right.

Telephone: 01277 841137.

How to get there: Stock sits on the B1007 on the hills between Billericay and Chelmsford. The Hoop is on the main street near the war memorial.

Parking: The pub has no car park as such, but unrestricted parking is available on the roadside near the pub. Otherwise you may park in the Square nearer the village centre.

Length of the walk: 4 miles. OS Map Landranger series 167 Chelmsford and Harlow (GR 693991).

A splendid short walk passing through as it does the grounds of the Catholic church and shortly after the parish church of Stock before descending to Ramsey Tyrrells Farm. From here to Fristling Hall there are wide views over the Wid valley. Soon after we have the climb from Swan Wood up to Crondon Park Lane and back to the delightful village of Stock.

The Walk
Leaving the Hoop turn left along the gravel path parallel to the main street. This is a good pedestrian way being segregated by some yards from the traffic. After reaching the Bear public house turn left along Mill Road passing on the way most of the handful of shops in Stock. Later you may wish to explore further along Mill Road, in particular the Tower windmill which stands on the eastern edge of the village and is probably the best in Essex, where most surviving mills are post mills. Soon cross the road to turn right into the footpath at the side of the Catholic church. In the early eighties the Stock parish priest was elevated to become Bishop of Brentwood. Follow the path through

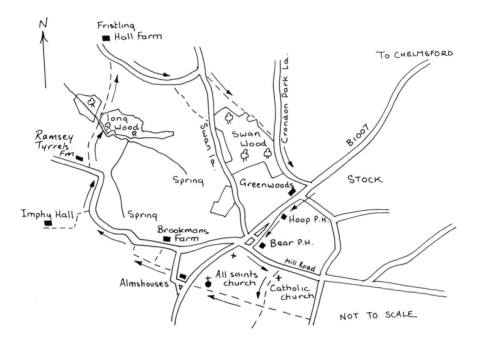

the grounds and after negotiating a kissing gate turn right (west) for about 200 yards to enter All Saints churchyard which leads to the main road. All Saints church is 14th century with a delightful wooden spire. The belfry is also wooden, indeed so huge are the curved beams that the biggest oaks in the forest must have been felled for them. The belfry is in fact older than the church.

On the opposite side of the road are a row of almhouses built by Richard Twedye in the 17th century for four knights fallen on hard times. Cross the road passing the almhouses and turn right up School Lane. Just round the corner at a footpath sign turn left along the right hand side of a house soon crossing a stile into a field. Continue to the next crossing hedge and cross another stile. To your left are wonderful views. In the foreground is South Hill Farm. To the south is Billericay and to the south west is Mountnessing church. After walking on for a further 200 yards, cross through the hedge on your right over another stile. Now walk on in your new direction (north east) for 130 yards to a lane. Turn left and follow this lane round right and left bends to Ramsey Tyrrells farm. Just past the first barn turn right and walk across a field (north) to a gate. Go through this into the next field and walk uphill.

At the top of the hill keep the hedge on your left and cross a stile and a gate out of the next field to reach a farm road to the right of Fristling Hall Farm. Here turn right and follow this farm road for about 300 yards to a road. If you cross this road just to the left a footpath sign directs you to the right (south east). Soon you are walking close to Swan Wood. You may encounter a boggy area. Cross this carefully and climb the last 150 yards to reach a house on Crondon Park Lane. Now turn right and follow this lane round the field through a farm steading to the main road at Stock. Turn right and in another 200 yards you arrive back at the Hoop.

Stondon Massey
The Bricklayers Arms

Stondon Massey is famous for having been the village home of the father of English music, William Byrd, who lived in Stondon Place from 1593 till his death in 1623. By the way, the village name reminds us that this stony hill belonged to the Marci family who came from Normandy, and that explains why the charming little church is Norman.

I have memories of 'The Brick' for many years and for the last 19 of them Keith and Sue Gardner have been the licensees. It is a wonderful pub with a wide range of clients. Keith himself has a large following and had been inclined to get up to unexpected exploits over the years. There was the time one Christmas morning when for charity he swam a length of the village pond which is opposite.

One of the excellent Grays houses, the Bricklayers serves Greene King IPA and Abbot real ales. Children and dogs · are welcome providing their behaviour is reasonable. We do not recommend you to emulate even in the summer the swim in the pond.

Most of the food is home-made and various delicious specialities are recommended. Opening times are 11.30 am-3 pm and 5 pm-10.30 pm Monday to Friday, 11.30 am-11 pm Saturday, and 12 noon-10.30 pm Sunday.

Telephone: 01277 821152.

How to get there: Stondon Massey is signposted off the A128 at Marden Ash near Ongar and at Fox Hatch 2 miles north of Brentwood. It is also signposted at Norton Heath off the A414. All routes lead to the pub with a pond and green opposite.

Parking: At the pub. Please ask permission before you leave for your walk.

Length of the walk: 3 miles. OS Map Landranger series 167 Chelmsford and Harlow (GR 586004).

Where else on a short walk can you encounter a whipping post, the residence of a world famous musician — now owned by a former world snooker champion — and a village pond where daring feats took place, all on a 'stony hill'? This is a charming little walk, and one which will draw you back to this magic village.

The Walk

Leave the pub and cross the main road to the concrete footpath sign heading south west between the house and the bungalow. This path leads beside the bungalow back garden and out to a field. Look for the yellow waymark arrows on the 3 ft post. As you go into the field turn right and walk behind the houses on a well marked path dipping down as you near the hedge. Cross the dip to the far side of the hedge and immediately turn left with the hedge on your left and walk south west until it ends, then cross a wire fence and enter a field. Continue in a south westerly direction towards the chestnut trees, the tops of which can be seen on the horizon. As you reach the junction of two paths head for the gap in the hedge ahead near the base of the chestnut trees. Once out of this field turn right and continue north west near the ditch on your right. Head for the earth bridge ahead and cross the little stream.

Walk slightly uphill towards the road in a north westerly direction to the right of Stondon Place ahead. Take care as you approach the road. When you reach it head left to the road junction. Here examine the whipping post. In years gone by those citizens who offended the rules of the land found themselves trapped and sometimes taunted for their crimes whilst unable to defend themselves. Let the children try out the restrictions and imagine what may have been their just reward if found guilty of a crime – but enough of make believe.

Return a few steps and look for another footpath sign across the road to the north. Cross the stile and follow the uneven path between two fences to the left hand corner of the wood ahead. When you reach the wood look over to your left (north west) towards Stondon Hall and church. But for the concerted action of local villagers as well as the Ramblers' Association, gravel works would be coming to the doorsteps of these two buildings. Continue down the left hand side of the wood to cross a stile and bridge which negotiates the hedge line ahead. Head up the hill, crossing diagonally to follow the fence on your left out to the road (Woolmongers Lane). Turn slightly left and look for a footpath sign on the right. Cross the stile and keep to the right of the field, passing a farmhouse two fields away on your left.

After passing a pond turn immediately left and cross the stile at the back of the pond. Beware of damp patches underfoot. Turn immediately right and keep to the field edge, heading for the gap at

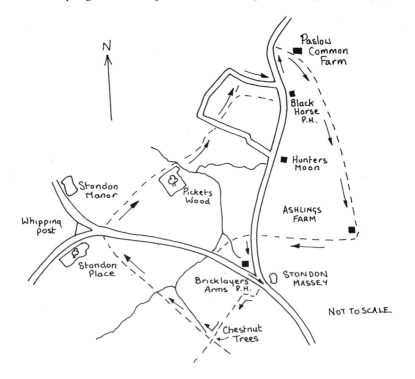

the right hand end of the hedge ahead. Cross this field and go over the next stile and bridge to rejoin Woolmongers Lane. Turn right and follow the lane out to Nine Ashes Road. Now turn left for a few yards and at a footpath sign turn right along the farm drive of Paslow Common Farm. Just past a house bear right with a fence on your right to a gate. Go through the gate and pass the ends of the gardens of the houses on your right. Continue along the field but, before coming to the very large house on the right, the path leaves the hedge line to head across the field southwards downhill to Ashlings Farm. Pause to look left for a glimpse of Blackmore church far away to the east.

On reaching the farm go through the white gate and cross the brook bridge to enter a small paddock. Go straight on across the paddock and head slightly right onto a tree lined track between the houses. Look for a post with arrow markers on it. At this point turn right and cross a plank bridge. Continue along a field edge with a hedge on your right to the end of the field and look for the plank bridge to enable you to cross the hedge line into a large field. Here the cross-field path is regularly walked so you should have something visible to follow. Make your way to the right hand edge of the houses and arrive at Nine Ashes Road. Now turn left and soon you will pass the village green on your left and regain your car at the Bricklayers Arms.

Tillingham
The Cap and Feathers

Tillingham (which means of the people of Tilli) is an ancient settlement. In AD 610 the manorial rights were given to the Dean and Chapter of St. Pauls who own the property to this day. A very nice village street widens, just south of the Norman church of St. Nicholas, into a green, and there are many pretty weatherboarded cottages.

The Cap and Feathers is the only house owned by the small Essex brewer – Crouch Vale. It is undoubtedly one of the finest pubs in the county. Part of the building dates back to 1425, but most of it is Elizabethan. You will hear about the ghost, only ever seen at breakfast time in the bar. He is dressed in sailor's clothing, and has been named 'Captain Cook'. Opening times are 11 am-2.30 pm, Mondays to Fridays, 11 am-3 pm on Saturdays, and 12 noon-3 pm Sundays. Evening times are 6 pm-11 pm Mondays to Saturdays and 7 pm-10.30 pm Sundays. Food is served 12 noon-2 pm and 7 pm-9 pm, and until 8.30 pm on Sundays. There is no food on Mondays. Specialities are home-made pies like Tillingham pie made with beef and Crouch Vale beer.

Real ales are Woodham IPA, Best Bitter, SAS, Willie Warmer plus a guest beer, changing each week. Traditional Somerset cider is on draught. There is a small beer garden at the rear and a children's room. Well behaved dogs are welcome. The Cap and Feathers also offers bed and breakfast accommodation.
Telephone: 01621 779212.

How to get there: Make your way to Latchingdon from Maldon or South Woodham Ferrers. Now follow the signs to Mayland and Steeple. On your way to Bradwell, turn right at the boarded up Queens Head. When you reach Tillingham pass the church, and the Cap and Feathers is 130 yards further on the right.

Parking: The pub has a good car park in Vicarage Lane. If you want to leave your car there while you walk, please ask the landlord.

Length of the walk: 4½ miles. OS Map Landranger series 168 Colchester and the Blackwater (GR 993037).

A visit to Tillingham, a stroll by Stows Farm through the picturesque lakes to reach the spectacularly sited St. Lawrence church, with views over the estuary, before returning by St. Peters Way past West Hyde and East Hyde, through Tillingham sports fields to St. Nicholas church, makes a splendid two hour walk. If you also take the opportunity of visiting St. Peter's Chapel you will have had a fine introduction to the Dengie peninsula where the land is fertile and the people sparse.

The Walk

Leaving the pub turn left and walk along Vicarage Lane. Pass a sports ground on your right. Between the cricket pavilion and another building is a water pump with a slate roof, renovated in 1985 in remembrance of a lady who so loved the peace of the village. Next we come to three delightful thatched cottages, and finally the vicarage, unfortunately empty. About 150 yards on we arrive at Stows Farm – very neat and tidy and with a small aeroplane in the back yard. A large pedestal attests to an award by the Sand and Gravel Association for the restoration work done here on the gravel pits. Certainly the area of ponds, bushes, and swans is a tranquil sight, although slightly marred by frequent 'keep out' notices.

The footpath from the farm is a good track to the lane – Reddings Lane. Turn left and right at the black footpath sign and follow a grass track with the hedge on your right. After 600 yards the defined path turns right into the next field. You carry straight on. At the field corner turn left for a few yards to cross the hedge line and continue (west) to join a bridleway track coming in from the left. Just before the pylon

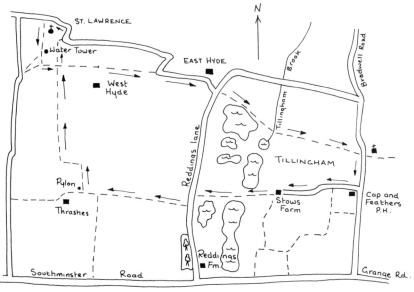

NOT TO SCALE

and near the white house named 'Thrashes', turn right across a field passing under the overhead wires as you walk north. Here the bridleway has been diverted round the field edge. You turn left and then right in the corner to follow the hedge all the way, finally turning right to the concrete bridleway sign by the road. Turn left again and follow the road round to St. Lawrence church. Here admire the views – the Blackwater estuary, Osea island to the left, and on a fine day Tollesbury, and West Mersea to the right.

From here walk through the farmyard. When you come to a field observe that two footpaths meet by the road to your half right 250 yards away. By taking a courtesy path round the left edge of the field you can join the second path at a gap in the hedge on your left. Here turn left to follow the hedge on your left in the next field. You are now on the St. Peters Way, a long distance path from Ongar to Bradwell.

At the end of this field cross a plank bridge and continue east to the hedge corner by West Hyde. Keep the hedge on your right to the corner of a road. Now walk along this road (east). Soon you will pick up an old wooden footpath sign, and follow this path near a large pond, crossing Tillingham Brook by a bridge. Very soon you arrive at the north side of the playing fields. Follow these to the church. Now turn right for 130 yards and arrive back at the Cap and Feathers.

122

A visit to Tillingham should be followed by a 3 mile drive along the road to St. Peter's Chapel. Take the signs to Bradwell village and turn right past the church. The last ½ mile or so is only accessible by foot and soon you come to the tiny chapel built in AD 653 by Cedd, who first brought Christianity to England. Go inside the chapel and experience the sense of timelessness. What is striking is that with all the simplicity of St. Peter's Chapel it can only be described as beautiful. Reflect on your visit here as you retrace your steps to the car – was it not unforgettable?

Woodham Walter
The Cats

Woodham Walter is a small parish situated about 2½ miles west of the ancient town of Maldon. Last century the population comprised gentry, farmers, and workers. Nowadays only a minority of residents are connected with the land, most being business and professional people. Over hundreds of years settlements have developed at a number of points such as Spring Elms, Little London and Curling Tye Green. Woodham Walter epitomises all that is best in our county of Essex. There are the ancient shady woodlands of the common, the Wilderness, and several other woods, the rolling fields with open skies, and long views, and the more intimate scenery of the river meadows.

The Cats became a beer house in the early part of the 19th century. The original building dates back to the early 16th century. The interior is delightful with low beams and open fires, and the pub is justifiably popular, attracting a large number of regular customers. Opening times are 6 pm-11 pm on Mondays to Saturdays, 7 pm-10.30 pm on

Sundays. The Cats also opens on Thursdays to Sundays from 12 noon-3 pm. Food is on offer at lunchtime on Thursday to Saturday – just sandwiches and ploughman's, but made with crusty fresh bread and ingredients each day. Real ales available include Greene King IPA, Abbot, and guest beers, all excellently kept. Children are accommodated in a splendid garden. All in all the Cats is a gem. Go there at certain times of the year and you will see on display some of the landlord's collection of steam engines, fairground organ, and classic cars.

How to get there: Woodham Walter is signposted from the A414 Chelmsford to Maldon road just east of Danbury. When you reach the village go through, passing the church and the school. Right at the end of the village turn right on a road signposted to Curling Tye Green. The Cats is 600 yards along this narrow lane on your left.

Parking: Park at the pub, but please ask the landlord before setting out on your walk.

Length of the walk: 3 ¾ miles. OS Map Landranger series 168 Colchester and the Blackwater (GR 815076).

This walk takes you round the environs of some historic parts of what is undoubtedly a beautiful parish. Few are the remains of Woodham Walter Hall which experts tell us would probably have been like Kentwell Hall in Suffolk.

The Walk
From the Cats walk out to the road, turning left along Blue Mill Lane for 300 yards. Now turn right into Whitehouse Farm. The farm buildings are sadly disintegrating – some years ago this farm was bought for gravel but planning permisson was not granted so the land is farmed by others. Follow the track out of the steading going south. There is a ditch on your right and you soon come to a waymark post which indicates a crossing path. Continue from here to the ditch corner, a distance of some 550 yards. Now turn half right and walk towards the woodland known as the Wilderness. Follow on with the trees on your right. This was the site of Woodham Walter Hall which has long since gone. It is thought that when William Fytche married Elizabeth Cory in 1695 they went to live in Danbury Park and the old house in Woodham Walter was pulled down soon afterwards.

Walk on past two cottages and cross the road (Old London Road) into Lodge Farm. Follow the waymarks to the right of the buildings through a gate and over a stile to join the farm track at the south end of

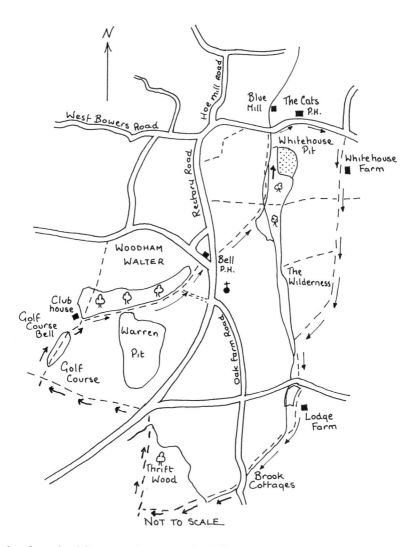

NOT TO SCALE

the farm buildings, and turn right following a hedge and stream on your right. Walk through a crossing hedge and over a plank bridge to a footpath post by the road. Cross the road and join a footpath by Brook Cottages past a large pond. When a stile appears on the left, turn right to a wood (Thrift Wood). Enter the wood walking west and follow the park to reach a wide track running north/south through the wood. Turn right (north) and follow the path to a road. Opposite the entrance to the Warren Golf Club cross the road and take the bridleway path which runs along the south west side of the course. Some 500 yards after leaving the road you come to a stile on the left. Here care is necessary. Turn right and cross a fairway past a green to find a path going through a little wood. At the other end cross another fairway to pick up the track running east from the clubhouse. Follow this track passing on your right a large gravel pit. About 650 yards from the clubhouse when the track bears right, carry straight on through a gap in the hedge, and walk downhill through a playing field to a concrete footpath post opposite the Bell public house. In the early 1900s Henry Thomson bought the Warren. He set about creating a golf course, and cricket ground. He also created playing fields above the Bell. On his death the villagers were delighted to learn that he had left the fields to the parish with £50,000 for their upkeep, 'being desirous to carry on his benefaction for all time'.

The composition of church, houses and pub is striking. Here turn right and a short detour southwards will give you the opportunity to view the church which was built in 1563 by Thomas, Earl of Essex. This was the reign when churches fell into ruin, and very few were built. This one was deliberately constructed in the Gothic style although almost all buildings of the time incorporated Renaissance motifs. It is aglow with red bricks and has a red tile roof. Some treasures have been saved from its predecessor, including the font, tall and light with traceried panelling of the 15th century. There is medieval glass in the windows, and a bronze against the wall symbolising the work of the 20th century.

Retrace your steps to the road junction and turn right just beyond it by a footpath sign. At the end of the field cross over a stile into a wooded area, walking to the right of a little stream. You come to two concrete bridges. Cross the first and turn right briefly before turning left to again follow the stream, but not so closely, all the way back to Blue Mill Lane. Turn right up the lane for 250 yards to arrive back at the Cats.